THE CLUBS

An inside look at Major League Baseball's 30 teams.

Baseball Insiders Library®

THE CLUBS
An inside look at Major League Baseball's 30 teams.

THE CLUBS
An inside look at Major League Baseball's 30 teams.

Printed in 2012

ACKNOWLEDGEMENTS
Major League Baseball would like to thank Pat Kelly and Milo Stewart Jr. at the National Baseball Hall of Fame and Museum for their invaluable assistance; as well as Eric Enders and Paul Boye for their diligent work in helping to prepare this book for publication.

MAJOR LEAGUE BASEBALL PROPERTIES

Vice President, Publishing
Donald S. Hintze

Editorial Director
Mike McCormick

Publications Art Director
Faith M. Rittenberg

Senior Production Manager
Claire Walsh

Managing Editor
Jon Schwartz

Senior Publishing Coordinator
Anamika Panchoo

Associate Art Director
Mark Calimbas

Project Editor
Jake Schwartzstein

Project Assistant Editor
Allison Duffy

Editorial Intern
Gerald Schifman

MAJOR LEAGUE BASEBALL PHOTOS

Photo Manager
Jessica Foster

Project Assistant Photo Editor
Andy Jacobsohn

MLB INSIDERS CLUB

Managing Editor
Jen Weaverling

Art Director
Brian Peterson

Proofreader
Travis Bullinger

2 3 4 5 6 7 8 9 10 / 15 14 13 12
Copyright © MLB Insiders Club 2012
ISBN: 978-1-58159-555-0

MLB Insiders Club
12301 Whitewater Drive
Minnetonka, MN 55343

CONTENTS

INTRODUCTION

SINCE THE TAMPA BAY RAYS AND ARIZONA DIAMONDBACKS CAME into existence in 1998, there have been 30 active clubs in Major League Baseball. Unbeknownst to most fans, that figure represents about 30 percent of the total number of franchises — 95 — ever to have been a Major League club, including in leagues that existed before the AL and NL. Granted, many of these teams were formed early in pro baseball's existence, and some of those dropped out after just a couple of games, but this fact still underscores the success that every Big League team — be it the New York Yankees or the Washington Nationals (formerly the Montreal Expos) — has had by not only surviving, but by thriving for so long.

Every franchise has its own unique past, but the formula for what makes each club great is similar — some combination of most, if not all, of the following: star players and coaches; success on the field; a devoted ownership; special personalities; fan-friendly and innovative ballparks; and, perhaps most importantly, a loyal and passionate fan base.

The Braves, first known as the Boston Red Stockings and one of just two remaining charter members of the original eight-team National League created in 1876 — the Cubs are the other — have played more games than any other baseball team ever. They have won more than 15 pennants thanks to the likes of Warren Spahn, perennial Cy Young contender Greg Maddux and fiery manager Bobby Cox — who finished with a career .556 winning percentage and ranks fourth all time with 2,504 victories overall. The club's most famous player, Hank Aaron, broke Babe Ruth's home run record amidst scrutiny unimaginable by anyone not named Jackie Robinson, while simultaneously bringing joy to two cities — Milwaukee and then Atlanta after the team moved in 1966. No other franchise can compare with the Braves.

Just as no other franchise can compare with the New York Yankees. Called the New York Highlanders when they first moved to New York in 1903, the Yankees have been the most dominant franchise in the game, with more than double the number of championships than any other club. They played in arguably the world's most famous stadium — Yankee Stadium — for 84 years, then opened an impressive new edition across the street, properly christening it with their 27th world title in 2009. Their list of legendary players stretches on seemingly forever, from the larger-than-life Ruth to the classy Joe DiMaggio to American icon Mickey Mantle to "The Captain," Derek Jeter. No other club can compare with the Yankees in terms of historical success.

When it comes to immediate success, no other club can compare to the Miami Marlins. Born in 1993, the Marlins became the quickest expansion team to win two world titles, doing so in 1997 and 2003. They won it mostly with star veterans the first time around, before winning a second time with players many fans had never heard of before the season began. Now with a beautiful new stadium of their own, they hope to bring even more success to South Florida while building an even bigger fan base.

Baseball is the most beloved sport in America, and Major League Baseball the world's oldest professional sports league. And what makes the league so special is its collection of clubs. Indeed, nothing else compares.

With the help of Edgar Renteria's walk-off base hit in Game 7 of the 1997 World Series, the Marlins became champions in just their fifth season of existence.

ARIZONA DIAMONDBACKS

BY WINNING A DIVISION TITLE in their second season and a world championship in their fourth, the Arizona Diamondbacks enjoyed more early success than any new Big League Baseball franchise since the Red Sox debuted a century earlier. After a 97-loss first season in 1998, Diamondbacks management decided that was enough losing. That offseason, Arizona acquired several players who would lay the groundwork for success. The cherry on top was Randy Johnson, who inked a five-year deal that remains one of the best free-agent signings in MLB history. The spindly, mullet-wearing strikeout machine won the Cy Young Award in each of his first four seasons in Arizona, and his D-backs tenure established him as arguably the greatest left-hander of all time.

Arizona's playoff debut in '99 ended on a walk-off homer by the Mets' Todd Pratt, but two years later, after trading for righty Curt Schilling, the club won it all. In an intensely exciting World Series against the Yankees, D-backs closer Byung-Hyun Kim suffered devastating blown saves in Games 4 and 5, but his teammates redeemed him in a classic Game 7 showdown. Facing Yankees legend Mariano Rivera after an Arizona rally tied it up, Gonzalez poked a ninth-inning bloop single that gave the D-backs a walk-off championship.

Arizona made it back to the playoffs in 2002 — losing in the division series — but the following years were lean until 2007, when the Snakes signaled a change in direction by switching their color scheme. The flashy purple-and-teal look of the cellar-dwellers was gone, replaced by the brick red of foundation building. This new Diamondbacks club, powered by dynamic young outfielder Justin Upton and other homegrown stars, won division crowns in 2007 and 2011, giving Arizona fans hope for more to come.

The D-backs won a world title in just their fourth year of existence and have been no stranger to the playoffs since then.

The D-backs first took the field in 1998 (top) with Buck Showalter in charge. Gonzalez's Game 7 bloop single sunk the Yankees in 2001.

ROAD TO GLORY

Having tangibly come into existence with the 1997 Expansion Draft, the Diamondbacks faced the challenge of competing with the rest of the NL while also having to win the hearts and minds of Arizona residents.

D-backs Owner Jerry Colangelo decided that winning quickly was the solution. The franchise targeted savvy veterans, such as Steve Finley and Luis Gonzalez, in the ensuing years. But the acquisition that loomed largest was that of pitcher Randy Johnson before the 1999 season.

"It legitimized everything the franchise was trying to accomplish," said pitcher Brian Anderson, picked in the '97 Expansion Draft.

Bolstered by these additions, the D-backs won 100 games in '99 en route to their first division crown. The club continued to load up on talent via trades and free agency, adding Mark Grace, Craig Counsell, Reggie Sanders and Curt Schilling over the next two years.

"The goal from the very first meeting of Spring Training 2001 was to win the World Series," Grace said.

Although the dominance of Johnson and Schilling, who would combine for 43 wins while ranking first and second in strikeouts and ERA in the NL, respectively, was expected, Gonzalez turned heads with 57 homers. After a surprising division title and league pennant, only the Yankees, who won the previous three World Series, stood in Arizona's way.

Schilling allowed just three hits in a 9-1 Game 1 blowout and, not to be outdone, Johnson hurled a shutout in Game 2. In the wake of the Sept. 11 terrorist attacks on New York and Washington, President George W. Bush threw out the ceremonial first pitch at Yankee Stadium before Game 3, which the Yanks won behind a strong outing from Roger Clemens.

Arizona nearly threw away the Series in the next two games, twice giving up ninth-inning leads to lose in extra innings, with closer Byung-Hyun Kim blowing both saves. But the D-backs, down 3 games to 2, returned home to Phoenix with Johnson and Schilling scheduled to pitch the final two games.

"They gave us two massive body blows," said Finley. "But on our plane ride home people were like, 'It doesn't matter.'" In Arizona for Game 6, the D-backs' bats went off for a Series-record 22-hit outburst in a 15-2 romp.

Game 7 proved a classic. Through five frames, starting pitchers Schilling and Clemens put up zeroes before Danny Bautista drove in Finley in the sixth to stake Arizona to a 1-0 lead. When Schilling came out to the mound for the seventh, he allowed three hits to even the score, 1-1. In the eighth, he yielded a tie-breaking blast to Alfonso Soriano, giving the Yankees a seemingly insurmountable lead with closer Mariano Rivera looming.

Rivera breezed through the eighth, but the D-backs fought back in the ninth. Mark Grace flipped Rivera's second pitch of the inning to center for a single. Manager Bob Brenly then had David Dellucci run for Grace and asked Damian Miller to bunt. The catcher sent the ball straight back to Rivera, who sailed his throw to second base into center field. With two on and no out, Bell pinch-hit for Johnson, sending another bunt at Rivera, who fired to third to get the lead runner.

With men on first and second with one out, Tony Womack hit an RBI double and Rivera then hit Counsell to

THE "BIG UNIT" AVERAGED 15 WINS
A YEAR OVER 19 SEASONS, ADDING
FOUR STRAIGHT CY YOUNG AWARDS
IN HIS FIRST FOUR YEARS WITH
THE DIAMONDBACKS FROM 1999–2002.

After a two-year stint with the Yankees, Johnson returned to Arizona in 2007 for two more seasons.

Between their final playoff appearance of the championship era in 2002 and their re-emergence in 2011, the D-backs reached the postseason one other time, when they beat the Rockies on Sept. 28, 2007, to win the division crown (above). They would ultimately bow out in the NLCS.

Diamonds in the Rough

47,484 FANS packed into Bank One Ballpark (now Chase Field) on March 31, 1998, for the D-backs' debut — a 9-2 loss to the rival Rockies.

57 HOME RUNS smashed by Luis Gonzalez in 2001, a club record.

23 WINS recorded by Curt Schilling in 2002, a career high. For the second consecutive year, Schilling finished as the runner-up in the Cy Young Award race to his rotation-mate, Randy Johnson.

100 WINS reached by Arizona on the final day of its second season. The Diamondbacks won the NL West by 14 games over the San Francisco Giants.

load the bases. With the infield drawn in, Gonzalez then blooped a single to center for the walk-off run.

During the Series, a banner displayed at Bank One Ballpark read "Yankees = History, Diamondbacks = Future." Maybe it was right. Although the veterans who brought Arizona its first title wouldn't be together much longer, the fans the franchise won over in 2001 were on the bandwagon to stay.

DESERT KING

Fitting for someone who grew to be 6 foot 10, Randy Johnson had a youth filled with people telling him that he should pursue basketball. He didn't disagree, playing in high school and briefly at the University of Southern California, where he also was a pitcher. On the court, he was just another tree-limbed hoopster. On the mound, though, he was an intimidator who seemed to reach out and touch home plate with each delivery.

After a trade in May 1989, Johnson earned a rotation spot with the Seattle Mariners in 1990. The "Big Unit" averaged 15 wins a year over the next 19 seasons, adding four straight Cy Young Awards in his first four years with the Diamondbacks from 1999–2002, when he established himself as the best player in club history. Johnson was particularly lethal in the 2001 Fall Classic, when he went 3-0 to help Arizona top the Yankees. In the deciding contest, he threw more than an inning of shutout relief one day after hurling 104 pitches in a start; for his efforts he was named co-MVP of the Series along with fellow ace Curt Schilling. Johnson surpassed 300 wins before retiring in 2009.

RAISING ARIZONA

The Diamondbacks carried a fresh energy into 2011. Arizona had lost more than 90 games in each of the previous two seasons, but team President Derrick Hall was determined to turn things around.

Hall's most important personnel decision may have been the hiring of Kevin Towers, who built four division winners and one National League championship team during his 14 seasons with the San Diego Padres, as general manager toward the end of the 2010 campaign. "Arizona couldn't have picked a better person to turn that franchise around," Yankees GM Brian Cashman said after the selection.

The Diamondbacks' newly minted GM hit the road with the team for the final two weeks of the 2010 season and liked at least one thing he saw; Towers quickly decided to bring back Kirk Gibson — a fiery on-field leader during his playing days who was promoted from bench coach to interim manager earlier in the summer — as the manager for the 2011 season.

"I told Gibby, 'The culture feels so bad here; it's just blah,'" Towers said. "I thought the best way of changing it was bringing in the right coaching staff." So, early that year, Towers and Gibson went about recruiting a plethora of proven coaches in 1979 American League MVP Don Baylor (hitting), Charles Nagy (pitching), Eric Young (first base) and Alan Trammell (bench), each of whom made at least one All-Star team during his playing days. The duo also retained Matt Williams (third base coach, formerly first base) and D-backs mainstay Glenn Sherlock (bullpen). "We've got guys that have won before," Towers said. "That was a way of starting to create a winning-type attitude."

At the same time, Towers upgraded the front office in a series of moves that included the addition of Ray Montgomery, who left the Milwaukee Brewers to become director of scouting. During the winter, the braintrust traded Mark Reynolds to Baltimore, subtracting large numbers of home runs but even more strikeouts from the batting order and giving the team a chance for defensive improvement. He also added closer J.J. Putz to solidify a bullpen that had been the worst in baseball. Watching clips of the starting rotation gave Towers reason for optimism: Ian Kennedy, Daniel Hudson and Barry Enright were all promising.

Star outfielder Justin Upton welcomed the injection of new faces under the new regime. "Gibson brings the intensity every day," he said.

Sure enough, the D-backs showed massive improvement in 2011, going from worst to first by winning 94 games a year after winning just 65. With a young team and plenty of young talent, sustained success has now become the expectation.

The swimming pool beyond the outfield fence at Arizona's Chase Field marks one of the more unique ballpark attractions that can be found anywhere around the Major Leagues.

ATLANTA BRAVES

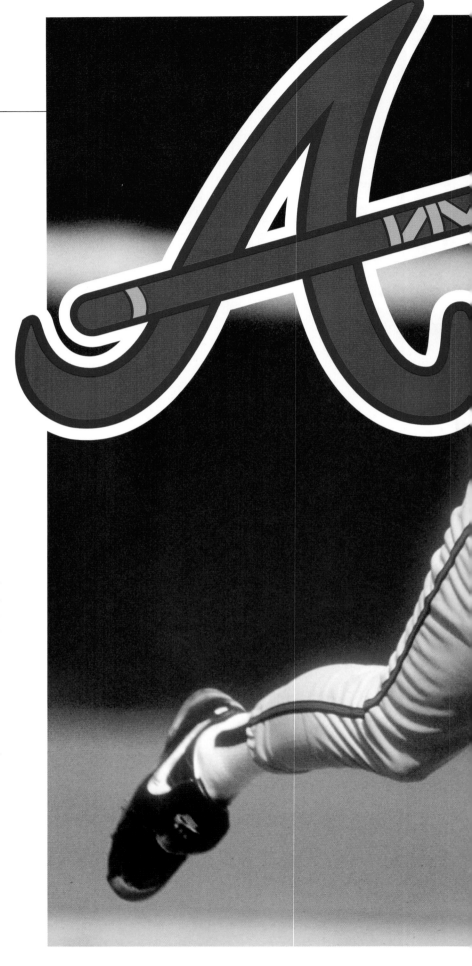

THE OLDEST FRANCHISE IN American professional sports, the Braves also had the game's first star, George Wright. Originally known as the Cincinnati Red Stockings, baseball's first pro team moved to Boston in 1871, where iconic shortstop Wright and his older brother, player-manager Harry, would lead the club to six pennants in seven years. Four decades later, then sporting a new nickname, the 1914 "Miracle Braves" authored what remains baseball's all-time underdog story: In last place as late as July 18, the ragtag club stormed to a 59-16 finish and swept the Philadelphia Athletics in the World Series.

The 1940s brought the franchise both a pennant and a famous saying ("Spahn and Sain and pray for rain"), but it was during the next decade that the Braves truly arrived. They sparked baseball's westward expansion by relocating to Milwaukee in 1953, where their two young superstars — Eddie Mathews and Hank Aaron — drew fans to County Stadium in massive numbers. Mathews clubbed 47 homers at age 21, while Aaron had led the league in each Triple Crown category by the time he was 23. Bolstered by the cagey southpaw Warren Spahn, the Braves became annual contenders and brought home Milwaukee's only title in 1957.

After the team's 1966 move to Atlanta, Aaron mounted an inspiring run at the career home run record held by Babe Ruth — who himself had hit his last homer as a Brave. After Aaron smacked his 715th longball in 1974, it was mostly dark days for the franchise. The early years of media mogul Ted Turner's ownership were marked by losing, often in comical fashion, but by the 1990s the Braves had laid the foundation of a model farm system and constructed one of the greatest baseball dynasties ever. With a stupendous rotation led by Greg Maddux, Tom Glavine and John Smoltz — 873 career wins and seven Cy Young Awards between them — Atlanta captured an incredible 14 division titles in 15 years.

A three-time Cy Young winner with the Braves, Maddux anchored Atlanta's rotation during the team's incredible run of success in the '90s. During his tenure, the Braves won nine NL East titles in the midst of a span that netted them 14 division crowns in 15 years.

During their time together, each of the pitchers won at least one Cy Young Award between 1993 and '98, including three claimed by Maddux, who had also earned the hardware in his final season with the Cubs in 1992 before coming to Atlanta.

Longtime Braves pitching coach Leo Mazzone held a front-row seat for the trifecta's show over the years and came away impressed by their commitment and passion for pitching. "Every day you'd appreciate it," he said. "You understand why some people have success and some don't. The biggest thing about their greatness is their consistency in all areas: Their approach, their preparation, their work ethic, their mental toughness. They're very special."

While Smoltz had a unique career path — going from Cy Young starter to All-Star closer and back to All-Star starting pitcher — Maddux and Glavine, born three weeks apart in 1966, enjoyed similar progressions. After posting identical 2-4 records in their first year in the Major Leagues, Maddux posted 20 consecutive seasons of double-digit wins, while Glavine rode a streak of 14 to total 18 in 19 seasons. Ultimately, both Maddux (355 victories) and Glavine (305) reached the coveted 300-win plateau, while Smoltz won 213 games to go along with his 154 career saves.

Best of the Decade

VICTORY LEADERS OF THE 1990s

1.	**Greg Maddux**	**176**
2.	**Tom Glavine**	**164**
3.	Roger Clemens	152
4.	Randy Johnson	150
5.	Kevin Brown	143
	John Smoltz	**143**
7.	David Cone	141
8.	Mike Mussina	136
9.	Chuck Finley	135
10.	Scott Erickson	130

ERA LEADERS OF THE 1990s

1.	**Greg Maddux**	**2.54**
2.	Roger Clemens	3.02
3.	Randy Johnson	3.14
4.	**Tom Glavine**	**3.21**
	David Cone	3.21
6.	Kevin Brown	3.25
7.	Curt Schilling	3.31
8.	**John Smoltz**	**3.32**
9.	Dennis Martinez	3.37
10.	Ramon Martinez	3.45

Smoltz received accolades as a Big League starter and reliever, amassing 213 victories as well as 154 saves during his career, 20 years of which were with Atlanta.

THREE OF A KIND

The Three Musketeers' Athos, Porthos and Aramis can't hold a sword to the Braves' tri-headed beast of Greg Maddux, Tom Glavine and John Smoltz that ruled pitching mounds throughout the 1990s and early 2000s.

In the years that the trio were teammates — from 1993–2002 — Maddux compiled 178 victories with the team, Glavine won 169 games, and Smoltz earned 106 victories despite missing all of the 2000 campaign with an injury and starting just five games from 2001–02, when he was converted to a relief pitcher and recorded 65 saves. Their 453 combined victories as teammates are the most ever.

Adept at painting the corners, Spahn was the original Braves ace. He owns the all-time record for wins by a left-hander.

SPAHN OF GREATNESS

"Hitting is timing," Braves Hall of Famer Warren Spahn once said. "Pitching is upsetting timing."

Spahn was already 25 before he won his first game, but became perhaps the greatest old-age pitcher ever, throwing two no-hitters and winning 20 games three times after his 39th birthday. One of the savviest hurlers ever, Spahn was famed for his memory and kept a mental book on every hitter he ever faced, storing information away for future use. It seemed that Spahn never made the same mistake twice.

"It's been 10 to 15 years since I've tried to overpower a hitter," he admitted late in his career. "I do business on the corners."

Spahn also was an excellent hitter. There are only about 100 players in history who have homered in at least 17 consecutive seasons. Jimmie Foxx and Lou Gehrig are not among them, but Spahn is, and his 363 career pitching wins are the most by any left-hander in history.

Originally built to host the 1996 Summer Olympic Games, Turner Field has been home to the Braves since 1997. Significant upgrades were made in 2005.

TEAM OF ALL '90s

After a brief playing career, Cox enjoyed two stints at the helm of the Braves, including one period of more than 20 years that encompassed the team's dominant run as the "Team of the '90s." He retired following the 2010 season.

The Atlanta Braves can be dubbed the "Team of the '90s," and for good reason. Not since the great Yankees dynasties has a team enjoyed a decade of season-to-season success akin to what the Braves achieved in the last 10 years of the 20th century.

But this dynasty was by no means the first in Braves history. In fact, Bobby Cox's team was not even the first Team of the '90s in the history of the franchise. A century ago, the Braves, then playing in Boston, dominated the 1890s. Just as the modern Braves won five pennants in the last decade of the 20th century, their Beantown ancestors won five pennants in the final years of the 19th century.

As the Boston Red Stockings, the club was a charter member of baseball's first professional league in 1871. Ever since then, whether in Boston, Milwaukee or Atlanta, the Braves franchise has fielded a team in every year of professional baseball.

By the 1890s, though, the glory of the Red Stockings had faded, and the squad was often known by its other unofficial nickname: the Beaneaters. But it was not long, says Boston baseball historian Frank J. Williams, before "the name became feared around the league. When the Beaneaters came to town, you knew you were really playing the best."

Under the guidance of Frank Selee, a proven Minor League skipper who inherited the Beaneaters' managerial duties in 1890, the club added legendary players like Kid Nichols and Billy Hamilton, key cogs for the team that would eventually topple the rival Baltimore Orioles for the pennant in 1897.

Some believe that the 1897 championship squad was the greatest of its century. The Beaneaters added luster to that claim by winning the rematch with Baltimore in 1898, taking the club's fifth pennant of that 10-year span.

Nonetheless, the 1890s were big enough to boast two great teams. Likewise, even though the Braves of the 1990s will have to share the decade's laurels with the storied Yankees, this fact should not overshadow their accomplishments as the club to beat, the franchise's second Team of the '90s.

Braves Hall of Famers

HANK AARON	Totaled 15 seasons with 30-plus home runs.
HUGH DUFFY	Finished with a .386 career OBP.
BILLY HAMILTON	Captured two NL batting titles.
RABBIT MARANVILLE	Stole 32 bases in 1916.
EDDIE MATHEWS	Launched 512 career home runs.
TOMMY McCARTHY	Collected 126 RBI in 1894.
CHARLES "KID" NICHOLS	Nailed down 361 career wins.
PHIL NIEKRO	Took the 1967 NL ERA crown.
FRANK SELEE	Led team to five pennants in the 19th century.
WARREN SPAHN	Threw no-hitters in 1960 and 1961.
VIC WILLIS	Won 27 games in 1899 and 1902.

Braves fans — shown here doing the "Tomahawk Chop" — have had plenty of star-laden teams to cheer for throughout the club's history.

THE HAMMER

Of all the men who have donned a Major League uniform, only Jackie Robinson is more revered than Hank Aaron. Under extreme scrutiny as a black ballplayer during the Civil Rights era, perhaps no player accomplished more. It's no accident that Aaron's statue stands outside Turner Field, which is situated at 755 Hank Aaron Drive. The number, of course, is no accident either.

Aaron hit 755 career homers in a Braves uniform, 733 of them spanning his first 12 seasons in Milwaukee and the next nine in Atlanta. The most spectacular of them all, his 715th, the one that surpassed Babe Ruth's career total, was hit in Atlanta, on April 8, 1974, on Henry Aaron Night. "Thank God it's over," an exhausted Aaron told a national television audience, referring to the emotional and physical ordeal of his pursuit of Ruth's mark. It was one of the great moments in baseball history, the video footage still eliciting chills.

In the time leading up to the home run, former teammate and Hall of Famer Eddie Mathews was prescient when discussing the chase for 715. "I don't know where Hank Aaron will break Ruth's record, but I can tell you one thing," he said, "10 years from the day he hits it, 3 million people will say they were there."

All of Aaron's numbers — not just 715 and 755 — are awesome. He's the Braves' career leader in numerous categories, including games played, at-bats, runs scored, hits, doubles, home runs, total bases, runs batted in, extra-base hits and stolen bases. No other player leads one team in so many batting categories — not Willie Mays, not Stan Musial, not Ruth, not Rogers Hornsby, not Ty Cobb, not *anyone*. Even after he turned 32, Aaron led the Atlanta Braves in home runs and RBI during each of the first six years of the franchise's Southern existence.

"As far as I'm concerned, Aaron is the best ballplayer of my era," three-time AL MVP Mickey Mantle once said. "He is to baseball of his era what Joe DiMaggio was before him."

Aaron (opposite) and Murphy were unrivaled during their respective careers in Atlanta, pacing the league in several stats and winning a host of awards. Although Aaron ended up in the Hall of Fame, Murphy took home two MVP Awards to Aaron's one.

TWICE AS NICE

Modest, principled and empathetic, Atlanta Braves center fielder Dale Murphy was more than just a great baseball player. Case in point: After winning his second consecutive MVP Award in the early 1980s, Murphy was typically humble. "It's a great compliment," he told *The New York Times*, "but I don't think you can pick an out-fielder to be the Most Valuable Player. I think a shortstop or a catcher is much more valuable."

Hard to blame voters for picking Murphy, though. He won the first of five Gold Gloves in 1982, belted 36 home runs and knocked in 109 runs. He was even better the following year, batting .302 with 30 steals and league highs in RBI and OPS. After Murphy was named the MVP in 1983, his manager showered him with praise.

"There was only one Henry Aaron and one Willie Mays," Joe Torre told *The Times*, "but Dale Murphy can do the things they could do."

BALTIMORE ORIOLES

NO BASEBALL FRANCHISE IS ever without hope, and the Baltimore Orioles are Exhibit A. After serving as an American League doormat for the first half of the 1900s as the St. Louis Browns — finishing in the bottom half of the league 38 times from 1901–50, employing a one-armed outfielder and a dwarf pinch-hitter and once drawing 386 fans to a game — a contender blossomed briefly in the 1920s thanks to George Sisler, the speedy, slick-fielding first baseman who batted .420 in 1922. That year, the Browns topped 90 wins for the first and last time. But Sisler soon suffered a crippling sinus infection that blurred his eyesight and left him a shell of the player he had been, and the Browns soon lapsed back into their losing ways. Their only pennant was captured during the war-torn 1944 season, when they capitalized on the absence of star players from other teams.

The franchise did, however, enjoy a stark turnaround after moving to Baltimore in 1954. In 1966, trade product Frank Robinson ushered in an era of dominance with his hustling, all-out style of play, and he captured the Triple Crown, to boot. The O's pitchers bulldozed through that autumn's World Series, holding the Dodgers scoreless over the final 33 innings of a four-game sweep. Brooks Robinson's clutch glove helped nab a second championship in 1970, and four 20-game winners brought another pennant in '71. All this was presided over by Manager Earl Weaver, the hot-tempered iconoclast who preached the gospel of pitching, defense and three-run homers. It was Weaver who made a shortstop out of an Oriole coach's son in 1982, helping to mold Cal Ripken Jr. into a legend, and setting up Baltimore for another two decades as one of baseball's most revered clubs.

Nicknamed "Gorgeous George," Sisler helped briefly turn the club — known then as the Browns — into a contender during the 1920s. He beat out Ty Cobb for the AL batting crown in 1920 and '22.

BUILDING BLOCKS

Oriole Park at Camden Yards opened its gates in 1992, and is best known for being the first of many "retro-modern" stadiums that were built around the Major Leagues in the ensuing 15-plus years. Located minutes away from Baltimore's famed Inner Harbor — and just two blocks from the birthplace of baseball legend Babe Ruth — the area surrounding the stadium offers plenty of beautiful sights.

Inside the ballpark, there are orange seats that denote landing spots for switch-hitting slugger Eddie Murray's 500th homer and franchise icon Cal Ripken Jr.'s 278th longball as a shortstop, a positional record. These quirks help make Oriole Park timeless and contemporary all at once. Beyond the right-field bleacher seats lies Eutaw street, which boasts a considerable amount of fanfare and features brass baseballs embedded into the sidewalk to mark spots where home runs have landed after clearing the right-field fence.

Oriole Park hosted more than 40,000 fans per game in its first nine years of operation, and in 2008, the park's 17th season, the 50 millionth fan to pass through the stadium's turnstiles made Camden Yards the fastest in Major League Baseball history to reach that lofty milestone. In fact, only Los Angeles's Dodger Stadium and the recently deconstructed Yankee Stadium have hosted more fans than Oriole Park since its opening in 1992. Included among those are the 46,272 fans who came to see Ripken break Lou Gehrig's consecutive-games-played mark on Sept. 6, 1995, just one of many historic moments at Oriole Park.

Soon after Camden Yards hosted its first game in 1992, it became the gold standard by which all "throwback" ballparks would be measured.

 Birds of a Feather

11 **FIRST-PLACE VOTES** received by Boog Powell in the 1970 AL MVP race. The first baseman won it over a set of Twins (Tony Oliva and Harmon Killebrew).

4 **PITCHERS** combined to throw a no-hitter on July 13, 1991. Starter Bob Milacki left in the seventh after being struck by a line drive, and three relievers finished the game.

48 **WINS** recorded by the 1901 Milwaukee Brewers, the original Baltimore Orioles. When the franchise moved to St. Louis the following year, the team's record improved greatly. The club won 78 games and finished second in the AL.

147 **GAMES** won by Mike Mussina as an Oriole from 1991–2000. Known as a great fielder, Moose also earned four Gold Gloves during those years.

1.005 **WHIP** posted by Mike Cuellar during his 1969 Cy Young season. With a 23-11 record, he tied Denny McLain for the top AL pitching honor.

3 **HITS** allowed by Baltimore's Ray Moore in a complete-game shutout on June 28, 1957. Orioles starters combined to throw four such starts in a row in late June that season, ending with Moore's win over Cleveland.

LEGACY OF GREATNESS

Cal Ripken Jr. grew up in the world of baseball, following his father to various Minor League managerial outposts. By the time he made his Major League debut with the Baltimore Orioles on Aug. 10, 1981, he was already a second-generation baseball lifer at age 20.

The O's envisioned the younger Ripken, their second-round pick in the 1978 draft, as a third baseman. Even though he batted just .128 in a 23-game stint in '81, the team traded veteran Doug DeCinces to the Angels before the 1982 season to free the position for its youngster.

On Opening Day against the Royals, Ripken went deep and finished 3 for 5, before going 4 for his next 55. Manager Earl Weaver sat him for the second game of a

doubleheader on May 29, 1982. Ripken was back in the lineup the following day, and he wouldn't miss a game for the next 16 years — a streak of 2,632 contests.

On July 1, 1982, Ripken was penciled in at shortstop. Standing 6 foot 4 and weighing 225 pounds, Ripken was anything but the prototype for the position. But he went on to bat .264 for the season with 28 homers and 93 RBI. He also won the Rookie of the Year Award, setting the stage for not just a memorable season, but also an unforgettable career.

Said Ripken, "If you ask me what I think my legacy will be, I don't know. But I can tell you what I want it to be: 'He was a gamer.' I want people to think of me as someone who came to the ballpark every day and tried hard to meet every challenge."

Fans showed Ripken some love on Sept. 6, 1995, when he passed Lou Gehrig's record by appearing in his 2,131st straight game.

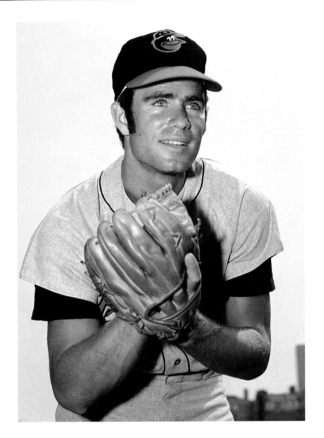

FOUR OF A KIND

Starting pitchers Palmer (left) and Dobson formed half of the Orioles' storied 20-victory rotation in 1971.

Although the Orioles won the World Series in 1970, their rotation accomplished something even more impressive the following season that hasn't been achieved since. For the first time in baseball history, a club boasted four 20-game winners.

While it's important to remember that the general approach to pitcher use in the 1970s varies significantly from the era of bullpen specialists seen in today's game, what the four Baltimore horses accomplished in 1971 remains an incredible feat. Although some foursomes have been expected to challenge that accomplishment — most recently, the members of the 2011 Philadelphia Phillies rotation — none have succeeded.

In 1971, Mike Cuellar, Pat Dobson, Jim Palmer and Dave McNally combined for 142 starts (and one relief appearance), 1,081 innings, a 2.89 ERA and, most famously, 81 wins against just 31 losses. Three of the four

notched at least 18 complete games, and even the low man of the group, McNally, had 11 to his name; just two pitchers since 2000 have thrown at least 10.

The Orioles rode their glut of pitching to 101 wins, the playoffs and an ALCS sweep of the Oakland A's. As good as their stable of arms was, though, the Orioles couldn't knock off the the Pittsburgh Pirates, who captured the crown in a thrilling seven-game World Series.

Combined, the four hurlers would have seven more 20-win seasons during the rest of their careers, and six of those would come from Palmer. In fact, the Orioles franchise saw just 13 total 20-win seasons from that historic 1971 campaign through 2011, further testament to the achievement that season.

Despite losing the Series in 1971, Cuellar, Dobson, Palmer and McNally each would make All-Star squads throughout their careers. Palmer had his No. 22 retired by the Orioles in 1985 and was inducted into the Hall of Fame in 1990.

THE ROBINSONS

In the early 1900s, when bunts were far more common, third base was quite possibly the most important defensive position in fair territory. Over time, heavy hitters replaced glove men at the hot corner, but Brooks Robinson's play in the 1960s was a throwback to the third basemen of the Deadball Era.

"Eight out of 10 times, I can tell when a man will bunt," Robinson said. "Most batters tip off their bunt attempts. When the pitcher throws, my body is in motion toward the plate. It's kind of like standing on a wall and seeing how far you can move forward without falling off."

Robinson was helped by being virtually ambidextrous; though he threw with his right hand, he did almost everything else in life left-handed, giving him added dexterity in his glove hand. The high point of Robinson's career came during the 1970 World Series, which he single-handedly dominated with a dazzling array of diving plays, back-handed stops and double plays. "Playing third is almost like being goalie on a hockey club," he said. "You aren't responsible for much ground, but you need quick reflexes and you have to be willing to stick your chin out in front of the ball if necessary."

Brooks' teammate with the same last name, Frank Robinson, did things a little differently. During the course of his 47 years in baseball, Frank played the role of wide-eyed rookie, tough guy, revered veteran, barrier-breaking manager and harsh disciplinarian.

After reaching the Majors in 1956 with the Reds, Robinson earned a reputation as a fearless and aggressive baserunner, especially because he went to great lengths to break up double plays. "If you can't break up a double play, knock the man down anyhow," he said in 1963. "Make him think a little the next time you come around."

As much as opposing players feared Robinson, his teammates greatly respected him. He was the undisputed leader of the Orioles after joining the club in 1966, league MVP and paternal figure to young players.

Whispers began as early as when Robinson was just 27 years old that he would become baseball's first African-American manager, and in 1974, at 38, he was named to helm the Cleveland Indians as a player-manager. He even hit a home run in his first game in his new role.

Robinson paced the Major Leagues seven times in the hit-by-pitch category, and he ranked among the league

Frank Robinson (above) swung a lethal bat and was one of the game's most feared sluggers. Brooks Robinson was known more for his glove, but he also hit above .285 six times and won an AL RBI crown.

leaders in that mark for 16 consecutive seasons, helped by a batting stance that placed his feet just three inches from home plate and left his arms squarely in the heart of the strike zone. Fittingly for a ballplayer who got beaned so often, he served as baseball's master of discipline from 1999–2001. It's the story of Frank Robinson's life — for every time he got knocked down, he would just get up and keep on going.

BOSTON RED SOX

THE FIRST 20 SEASONS OF THE Red Sox's existence were exquisitely memorable, and the most recent era has been, too. It's the in-between that New Englanders would just as soon forget.

During the franchise's debut season in 1901, Boston took a chance on 34-year-old Cy Young, a fading legend whose career appeared stalled. Over the next four years, Young posted a 1.96 ERA and averaged nearly 30 wins per season, leading Boston to their first-ever World Series title. Four more championships followed between 1912 and 1918, powered by five-tool center fielder Tris Speaker and then-pitcher Babe Ruth. In a risky move requiring extraordinary vision, Sox Manager Ed Barrow began playing Ruth in the outfield starting in 1918 — he would become a more permanent fixture there the following season — altering the course of baseball history.

The sale of Ruth to the Yankees prior to the 1920 campaign sent the Sox into a downward spiral from which they took decades to recover. The first step in that recovery came in 1941, when a cocky 22-year-old named Ted Williams hit .406. Williams would make the Sox a consistent contender during his career, but the team never got over the hump. Williams' successor, Carl Yastrzemski, won a pennant almost singlehandedly in 1967, but that "Impossible Dream" team also came up short in the quest to win the Fall Classic. So, too, did the 1975 squad, despite Carlton Fisk's homer in Game 6 of the Series.

In 1986 the Red Sox redefined heartbreak by coming within one strike of a championship, only to watch those hopes dribble away on a Bob Stanley wild pitch and a Bill Buckner error. Not until 2004 was the so-called "Curse of the Bambino" broken, when the plucky Sox rebounded from an imposing ALCS deficit to sweep the World Series. Another title followed in 2007, emphasizing that baseball's longtime underdogs — boasting splashy free-agent signings, vast monetary resources, and a ubiquitous television presence — had become the hunted.

From left: Ted Williams, Johnny Pesky, Bobby Doerr and Dom DiMaggio are honored with a statue outside Fenway Park. Unveiled in 2010, the statue was inspired by David Halberstam's 2003 book, *The Teammates: A Portrait of a Friendship*.

TEDDY BALLGAME

Williams was sometimes less than beloved by local fans, but his laser-focus on each at-bat made him arguably the best hitter the game has ever seen.

On July 22, 2002, more than 20,000 New Englanders gathered in Fenway Park to pay tribute to the greatest Red Sox player ever. With a zest for life matched by few human beings, Ted Williams enthusiastically dedicated himself to baseball, fishing, hunting, cooking, politics and innumerable other interests. While most ballplayers consider themselves lucky if they earn one nickname, Williams received four: The Splendid Splinter, Teddy Ballgame, The Thumper and The Kid.

For many years, Williams was a man of mystery; he did not want idolatry. Early in his career the media targeted Williams much as they did Albert Belle in the 1990s, which is a major reason why Williams failed to win the MVP in either of his two Triple Crown seasons. But over the next five decades his public image turned 180 degrees, and by the time he passed away on July 5, 2002, he had become a gregarious and engaging elder statesman.

Williams was famous for his oft-repeated wish to be remembered as the greatest hitter who ever lived, and today that is exactly the way most baseball fans think of him (even though the case for Babe Ruth may be a stronger one). And even if Williams was not the greatest hitter ever, he was surely the most intellectual. Williams never tired of discussing hitting, and never stopped trying to find ways to improve. He was the first batter to use rosin to improve his grip, and one of the first to realize that a heavier bat didn't necessarily lead to more home runs. While some great players prided themselves on being all-around performers, Williams did not. He focused on hitting and hitting only. He was famously stubborn, especially on the last day of the 1941 season, when he refused to sit on the bench to protect his .400 average, then went 6 for 8 in a doubleheader to raise the final figure to .406. It was a move that characterized Williams' entire life: Doing things his way, no matter what other people said, and usually succeeding tremendously.

Ortiz and the rest of the "Idiots" ended decades of dismay for Boston fans in 2004.

MENDED HEARTS

It was a moral victory when the Sox became the first team ever to force a Game 7 after trailing 3 games to none, as they did against the rival Yankees in the 2004 ALCS. It was an emotional victory to win that Game 7 and earn a spot in the Fall Classic. But moral and emotional victories wouldn't erase 86 years of frustration if the Red Sox had gone on to lose the World Series.

The St. Louis Cardinals entered the 2004 Fall Classic flying high, and they had history on their side, having defeated Boston in both previous World Series meetings (in 1946 and 1967). Coming in, the Cardinals' players were steady and professional, preferring to go quietly about their business. The Red Sox were loose and zany, befitting their self-imposed nickname, the "Idiots." It was a matchup between two classic franchises whose modern teams couldn't have differed more.

Even gutsier than the clutch hitting was the return of the red sock for the Red Sox. Curt Schilling, who underwent a minor but unprecedented surgical procedure to mend a tendon sheath in his right ankle before Game 6 of the ALCS against New York, repeated the ordeal for the World Series. After a high-scoring, 11-9 win for Boston in Game 1, Schilling threw six solid innings to win Game 2.

After another win in Game 3, the Red Sox scored in the first inning again in Game 4, the fifth contest in a row in which they got things off on the right foot. Johnny Damon was the catalyst, launching a leadoff homer off Jason Marquis.

Behind another strong effort from Boston pitcher Derek Lowe — who became the first pitcher to win three clinching games in a single postseason — the Red Sox would not yield en route to finally locking up a Series title, their first since 1918.

To the elation of New Englanders everywhere, the Red Sox had finally won it all. "I don't know exactly what this means [to fans]," Boston pitcher Pedro Martinez said, "but I have a feeling that there are a lot of people who can now die happy."

B Beantown's Best

34 **WINS** recorded by "Smoky" Joe Wood in 1912. The 22-year-old right-hander also posted a 1.91 ERA and whiffed a career-high 258. In the Fall Classic, he went 3-1.

105 **WINS** posted by Wood and the 1912 team overall — a franchise record. Led by Hall of Famer Tris Speaker at the dish, they finished 14 games clear of the Washington Senators for the American League pennant.

17 **RUNS** scored in one inning by the Red Sox on June 18, 1953, against the Detroit Tigers. Boston sent 23 hitters to the plate in the frame and racked up 14 hits and six walks.

20 **K's** tallied by burgeoning ace Roger Clemens on April 29, 1986, against Seattle. He was the first Major Leaguer to achieve the feat.

0.74 **WHIP** posted by Pedro Martinez in 2000, leading the righty ace to his second straight AL Cy Young–winning season.

2 **AWARDS** collected by Fred Lynn in 1975 — the MVP and Rookie of the Year. The center fielder teamed with left fielder Jim Rice to form one of the most prolific first-year duos ever.

BOSTON RED SOX

Dubbed a "lyric little bandbox of a ballpark" by John Updike in the pages of *The New Yorker*, Fenway fits in seamlessly with its neighborhood, offering locals an idyllic gathering spot since 1912.

HISTORY HAS BEEN EMBEDDED IN EVERY SQUARE FOOT OF FENWAY, FROM MOMENTS AND NAMES THAT DEFINE THE GAME'S HISTORY TO THE PRIVATE AND PERSONAL MEMORIES CHERISHED BY FANS.

AMERICA'S MOST BELOVED BALLPARK

Fenway Park has had plenty of renovations since it opened in April 1912 — the same week that the *Titanic* sank — but its famed features are instantly identifiable to fans.

What makes Fenway Park so unique and beloved is its history, a century-long tapestry of major renovations, ad hoc changes, subtle adjustments and stable periods spread across the decades. The ballpark's architecture has evolved organically over time, with new elements married to pre-existing irregular angles, strong steel girders and brilliant color schemes. The park seamlessly blends old and new, vintage and modern, classic and timeless. From its core design to its smallest details, the park reflects an enduring respect for tradition, combined with a renewed promise to best showcase the highest class of professional events.

Fenway Park is a living part of the neighborhood from which the venue takes its name. The surrounding streets bubble over with fans drawn to shops, bars and restaurants. Within the ballpark's intimate walls, microcosmic communities bustle, from the bleachers to the grandstands, from concourses and decks to private suites and clubs. Some of these areas have assumed the monikers of their corporate sponsors: the EMC Club, the State Street Pavilion, the Budweiser Roof Deck, the Coca-Cola Corner. Above all else, one truth predominates: The ballpark itself belongs to the community, and the Fenway Park name is not for sale.

In 2002, a new Red Sox ownership group led by John Henry, Tom Werner and Larry Lucchino sought to preserve and improve Fenway Park. With $285 million invested over the course of a decade in changes that touched every corner, the owners expanded and infused the space with 21st-century features to enhance the fan experience. Down to the smallest detail, the goal has been to retain the traditional, historical elements that make Fenway Park authentic and special. It's a unique situation for one of the game's most recognizable fields — maintaining that balance between old and new — that is necessary to keep Fenway's patina intact through the next generations.

To step into Fenway Park is to enter a world full of asymmetries and quirks: warped field dimensions, beguiling cavities, orphic nooks and, towering above everything else, the Green Monster. History has been embedded in every square foot, from epic moments and famous names that define the game's history to the private and personal memories cherished by fans.

Whether for a postseason clash (above) or for any other regular-season game, one truth is constant — there are few tougher tickets in sports than those to see the Red Sox play at Fenway. On Sept. 8, 2008, the Red Sox broke the Indians' record of 455 straight sellouts, a mark that seems certain to continue to grow as long as the team remains a contender in the competitive American League East.

GREEN WITH ENVY

As arguably the most famous landmark in American sports, the Green Monster has been the centerpiece of the best moment in club history, as well as its nadir. Just as Carlton Fisk is encoded in every Boston fan's DNA, so too is Bucky Dent.

Even if it has granted crafty hitters extra singles and doubles, the Green Monster has also denied many sluggers home runs, as shots that would fly out of other parks are stopped short by the wall's height. It's those hits that leave marks on the surface that add to the old ballpark's physical history, a living record of all the great hitters who have taken aim at Fenway Park's wall. "I know I left my dents," Red Sox shortstop Nomar Garciaparra said near the end of his Major League career.

Red Sox Hall of Famers

WADE BOGGS
Compiled 3,010 career hits.

JIMMY COLLINS
Raked at a .332 clip in 1901.

JOE CRONIN
Seven-time All-Star selection at shortstop.

BOBBY DOERR
Went 9 for 22 in the 1946 World Series.

RICK FERRELL
Retired with the most games caught (1,806) in the AL.

CARLTON FISK
Launched 351 career homers as a backstop.

JIMMIE FOXX
Won three MVP Awards and put up 30-plus longballs in 12 consecutive years.

LEFTY GROVE
Won 300 games and recorded a 3.06 ERA.

HARRY HOOPER
Hit .350 with two homers in the 1915 Series.

JIM RICE
Slugged 382 home runs and won an MVP Award in 1978.

TED WILLIAMS
Holds six career batting titles.

CARL YASTRZEMSKI
Totaled 3,419 hits and 452 home runs.

Young fans are as much a part of the Fenway lore as the famed wall.

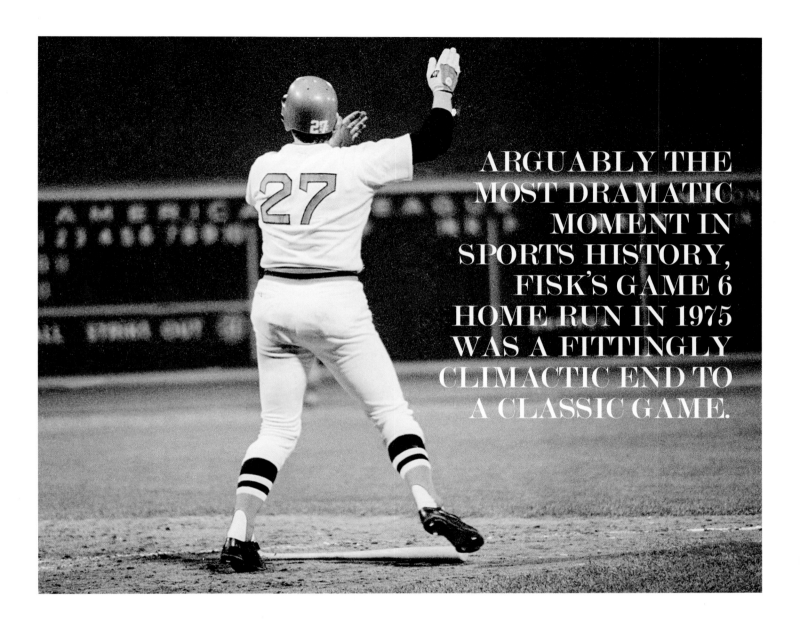

ARGUABLY THE MOST DRAMATIC MOMENT IN SPORTS HISTORY, FISK'S GAME 6 HOME RUN IN 1975 WAS A FITTINGLY CLIMACTIC END TO A CLASSIC GAME.

FAIR OR FOUL

The images from 1975 may represent the most famous and dramatic footage ever shot in a World Series game. Carlton Fisk connects with a 12th-inning pitch from the Cincinnati Reds' Pat Darcy. And then, as the ball heads toward left field, there's Fisk, using his best body English, willing the ball to stay fair, and as it ricochets off the foul pole, Fisk throws his arms up in triumph, leaping down the first-base line.

The shot of Fisk's reaction has become synonymous with Major League Baseball drama, and that Fall Classic as a whole is still considered one of the all-time greatest because of its many gut-wrenching and dramatic twists and turns over its seven games.

Still, Fisk might not have been the hero in Game 6 without a great play by right fielder Dwight Evans. With a man on first in the 11th, Evans raced back into the corner and hauled in a deep fly ball hit by Joe Morgan, robbing him of extra bases if not a home run. So it was still knotted, 6-6, when Fisk came to the plate and untied the game with his historic home run at 12:33 a.m., arguably the most exciting moment in sports history. It was a fittingly climactic end to a classic game.

CHICAGO CUBS

IT SAYS A LOT ABOUT THE CHICAGO Cubs' early years that despite not having claimed a championship since 1908, they have the second most total wins by any franchise ever. In fact, entering 2012, the Cubs were 532 games over .500. During the 1800s, under the ownership of sporting goods mogul Al Spalding, the club won six pennants behind the outstanding bat of Cap Anson. A few years later, an even better young Cubs team emerged. Forever memorialized in a poem, the most famous players were infielders Joe Tinker, Johnny Evers and Frank Chance, but the real star of the show was pitcher Mordecai Brown. The three-fingered hurler went 127-44 with a 1.42 ERA from 1906–10 as Chicago captured four pennants and a record 116 wins in 1906.

The Cubs weren't heard from again until the late 1920s, when they began winning pennants at three-year intervals — 1929, 1932, 1935 and 1938 — the last of these sparked by player-manager Gabby Hartnett's pennant-winning "Homer in the Gloamin'." Chicago lost the World Series each of those years, though, and again in 1945, when a tavern owner supposedly put a curse on the team for banning his pet goat from Wrigley Field. The Cubs haven't sniffed a pennant since, but that has never stopped North Siders from packing the Friendly Confines to cheer for the likes of Ron Santo, Ryne Sandberg and Sammy Sosa.

The Cubs of the 1960s featured four Hall of Famers, including Santo and Ernie Banks, the inimitable "Mr. Cub." But Banks, despite two MVP Awards and 512 career home runs, became something of a symbol of lovable losing. In 1969, his Cubs held a nine-game division lead on Aug. 17, only to fall victim to the Miracle Mets. Painful playoff losses followed in 1984, 1989 and especially 2003, when the Cubs came within five outs of the pennant before coughing up eight runs in the eighth inning of NLCS Game 6. These heartbreaks have caused Cubs fans to be more careful with their optimism — but that optimism could hardly be contained late in 2011 when the team hired Theo Epstein, the GM who broke Boston's curse, to serve as club president.

Throughout the past century, "The Friendly Confines" has been a bigger star than any one player. Still, greats such as Tinker, Evers and Chance (inset) have carved out a special place in Cubs lore.

43

THE FRIENDLY CONFINES

Hall of Fame shortstop Ernie Banks called the place "The Friendly Confines." Despite a lack of friendly postseason results, Wrigley Field — the second-oldest Big League park still in use (behind only Boston's Fenway Park) and the last one to install lights for night games, which happened in 1988 — has stood bounded by Clark and Addison streets and Waveland and Sheffield avenues on Chicago's North Side since 1914.

The facility was initially built for the Federal League's Chicago Whales, but the Cubs moved in two years later, naming the stadium after Owner William Wrigley Jr. in 1926. The Cubs drew 1 million fans during the 1927 season, the first NL team to do so.

The park's lively atmosphere extends well beyond its ivy-covered walls, into the surrounding neighborhood, dubbed "Wrigleyville," where fans can watch games from stands erected on the rooftops of buildings across the street.

The field has become famous for, among other things, its 27-by-75-foot hand-operated scoreboard behind the center-field bleachers, and the flags in center field. The "W" and "L" flags still alert local residents as to whether the Cubs have won or lost a game.

Wrigley Field's most well-known feature, the ivy that covers the outfield wall, actually hasn't been in the ballpark since the beginning. Bill Veeck, whose father had

been the club's president until his death in 1933, planted the green foliage in 1937.

Veeck planted 350 Japanese bittersweet plants to fill the space while 200 Boston ivy plants took root. His plan worked perfectly, but as the vines flourished, they became a bit of an issue for outfielders chasing balls that rolled to the wall. Sometimes players would reach down and pull up leaves instead of baseballs.

As a result of the dense outfield foliage, Wrigley was forced to develop some unique ground rules. If a ball is hit into the ivy and the outfielder can't find it right away, he is to put up his hands, signaling to umpires that the ball is lost. The batter is then awarded a ground-rule double.

But fielders at Wrigley must think quickly. If an outfielder attempts to make a play on a ball that has become caught in the ivy-covered wall, it's then considered to be in play. In that case, runners are entitled to take as many bases as they can while the fielder searches.

VOICE OF THE CUBS

With his huge glasses, funny opinions and boundless charisma, Harry Caray's larger-than-life personality entertained fans for the nearly 50 years that he spent broadcasting games for the Cardinals, White Sox, A's and Cubs. From his debut on KMOX in St. Louis in 1945, his enthusiastic style was unique, and he delighted fans with his trademark "Holy Cow!" exclamation of astonishment. Caray's passion was that of a fan, so when the team was great, he was over-the-top in his praise; when the team was losing, he let the players have it.

Caray began his career with the Cardinals, and after stops with the White Sox and A's, he found fame with the Cubs, becoming more popular than most of the players. He was the life of any party, whether it was arriving at the team's Spring Training facility on his golf cart with a cold beer in hand or mingling with fans in his unofficial role as "Mayor of Rush Street."

Later in his career, he became such a well-known figure that he was frequently imitated by players such as Will Ohman and Ryan Dempster, and actors like Will Ferrell, who would occasionally do a comical impression of Caray on *Saturday Night Live*.

"Harry was a man who celebrated life," said Steve Stone, former Big League pitcher and a longtime partner on Cubs broadcasts, after Caray's death in 1998. "He squeezed every iota out of the 80-some years that he had."

Veeck first planted the Wrigley Field ivy in 1937 when the ballpark was 23 years old. The leafy vines have been a fixture — as well as a defining trait — ever since.

C Chicago's Finest

41 **GAMES** combined over the .500 mark from 2007–08 for the Cubs. With Lou Piniella at the helm, Chicago won the NL Central both seasons.

8 **RBI** recorded by Ron Santo in the second game of a doubleheader on July 6, 1970. Santo, a nine-time All-Star and 2012 Hall of Fame inductee, hit two homers in the contest to help Chicago top the Montreal Expos.

3 **HOMERS** launched in one game on May 30, 1884, by Chicago's Ned Williamson against Detroit, the first three-dinger game in NL history. Williamson finished the season with 27 homers despite having never reached 10 any other year.

3.5 **INNINGS** played by the Cubs and the Phillies on Aug. 8, 1988, in the first night game in Wrigley Field history. Rainy weather canceled the park's debut under newly installed lights.

.378 **BATTING AVERAGE** posted by Derrek Lee in the first half of 2005. In one of the great starts in franchise history, Lee belted 27 homers and knocked in 72 runs before the All-Star break.

He may not be considered one of the most conventional announcers of all time, but few would deny that Caray was one of the most colorful characters the broadcast booth has ever seen.

GLOVE MAN

It was his bat that made Ryne Sandberg an MVP and a Hall of Famer. But his glove tells more about how super-human he could seem sometimes.

Sandberg won more Gold Gloves (nine) than any second baseman in National League history, finishing his career with the highest fielding percentage (.989) of anyone who manned the position in Major League history.

From 1989–90, he had the longest errorless streak (123 games) of any middle infielder in history. But while that was the streak that put him in the record book, it was simply typical of the way Sandberg played his position. Oh, and he held the all-time record for career homers by a second baseman (277) until Jeff Kent broke it in 2004.

And to think, this was a player who had to be convinced by his third manager in Chicago, Jim Frey, that he had something that could make him more than just a nice little second baseman; that he could be a middle-of-the-order thumper, an impact player, even an MVP (which he was, in 1984).

As it turned out, it was that Hall of Fame something. Sandberg proved he had that ingredient that eventually leads men, even those not originally stamped for stardom, down a country road in upstate New York to Cooperstown, where they find themselves surrounded by the greatest baseball players who ever lived.

MR. CUB

One day in the late 1950s, a young boy from Des Moines, Iowa, named Bill Bryson attended a Chicago Cubs game at Wrigley Field, where he encountered Cubs short-stop Ernie Banks autographing balls before the game. "Unbidden, I took it upon myself to sit beside him and pass him each new ball," wrote Bryson, who grew up to become a bestselling author. "This slowed the process considerably, but he gave a little smile each time and said thank you as if I had done him quite a favor. He was the nicest human being I have ever met. It was like being friends with God."

Displaying that sunny disposition virtually every day, Banks held court at the corner of Clark and Addison for 19 years, hitting 512 career home runs and endearing himself to Chicago fans as "Mr. Cub." At the height of his career, there was no better player in the game. Until Banks came along, no shortstop in baseball history had

ever hit 40 home runs in a season. Starting in 1955, he reached that milestone five times in six years. Using phe-nomenally strong, whip-like wrists, he powered his way to the MVP Award in both 1958 and '59, becoming the first National League player to capture those honors in back-to-back seasons.

As the first black player in Cubs history in 1953, he faced plenty of taunts and epithets from opposing fans and players. But instead of becoming bitter, Banks responded with kindness — not to mention ruthless production at the plate. By the late '50s, he was a valued mentor and one of the most respected players in baseball. "Ernie helped me more than anyone," Hall of Fame teammate Billy Williams said in 2008. "He was a trailblazer, and he always had fun playing this game."

The man who begged "Let's play two," Banks (above) was the first shortstop to hit 40 homers in a season, while Sandberg was a star with his glove.

AS THE FIRST BLACK PLAYER IN CUBS HISTORY, BANKS FACED PLENTY OF TAUNTS AND EPITHETS. BUT INSTEAD OF BECOMING BITTER, HE RESPONDED WITH KINDNESS.

"IT WAS ONE OF THOSE GAMES WHERE EVERYTHING YOU THROW WAS CROSSING THE PLATE. I WAS FOCUSED, THOUGH, SO I HAD NO IDEA HOW MANY GUYS I WAS STRIKING OUT." — *KERRY WOOD*

The fans in the bleacher seats beyond the outfield wall (right) always look for a reason to cheer, and Sammy Sosa's home run–hitting exploits during the late 1990s offered plenty of opportunities. The Wrigley Field message board above the entrance gate stands as one of the ballpark's most visible landmarks.

UNTOUCHABLE

On May 6, 1998, Kerry Wood began a game against the Astros by throwing a fastball to leadoff man Craig Biggio. The offering missed its target, and then some, plunking plate umpire Jerry Meals in the mask. It wasn't the most auspicious start, but the 20-year-old flamethrower from Texas eventually settled down and struck out the Astros' six-time All-Star.

Mixing nasty fastballs with vicious breaking balls, the rookie right-hander, in just his fifth Major League game, would strike out the side four times, finishing with 20 K's on the day. The only hit he allowed nicked the glove of Cubs third baseman Kevin Orie and could have been scored an error. Just one other batter reached base.

Wood broke numerous team and rookie strikeout records that day at Wrigley Field, among them the NL single-game record (previously 19) and the rookie benchmark of 18.

"It was one of those games where everything you throw was crossing the plate," Wood said. "I was focused, though, so I had no idea how many guys I was striking out."

Cubs Hall of Famers

CAP ANSON	Hit .399 in 1881 as Chicago's player-manager.
ERNIE BANKS	Led the league in homers and RBI twice.
MORDECAI BROWN	Showcased a devastating curveball.
FRANK CHANCE	Had a .394 career OBP.
KIKI CUYLER	Reached base 279 times in 1931.
JOHNNY EVERS	Pivot of the legendary double-play combination with Frank Chance and Joe Tinker.
GABBY HARTNETT	Hit 37 homers in 1930.
BILLY HERMAN	Master of the hit-and-run play.
FERGUSON JENKINS	Whiffed 3,192 men in his 19-year career.
MIKE "KING" KELLY	Won the 1886 batting title (.388).
RYNE SANDBERG	Hit at a .285 clip and was a natural fielder.
RON SANTO	Made nine All-Star teams and won five Gold Gloves at third base.
JOE TINKER	Had great speed and was a clutch shortstop.
BILLY WILLIAMS	Took home the 1961 Rookie of the Year Award and hit a total of 426 longballs.
HACK WILSON	Drove in 350 runs from 1929–30.

CHICAGO WHITE SOX

*T*HE FLAGSHIP FRANCHISE OF the American League during its infancy, the Chicago White Sox won the first two AL pennants in 1900 and '01. A decade later, they became occupants of the world's largest ballpark when lavish Comiskey Park opened on Chicago's South Side on July 1, 1910.

Led by the hitting of Shoeless Joe Jackson and the all-around excellence of second baseman Eddie Collins, the White Sox captured the club's second World Series title in 1917. But two years later, motivated by internal team squabbles and what they viewed as Owner Charles Comiskey's miserliness, seven Chicago players agreed to throw the World Series on behalf of gamblers. Despite being acquitted of any charges in a 1921 grand jury trial, all seven "Black Sox," plus non-conspirator Buck Weaver, were banned from baseball for life.

The suspensions gutted the roster and demoralized Sox fans, and for the next 35 years, Chicago never finished higher than third place. But in 1959, an exciting young team run by innovator Bill Veeck — who installed an exploding scoreboard at Comiskey Park in 1960 — captivated fans with crazy promotions and winning baseball. Energized by speedy infielders Nellie Fox and Luis Aparicio, the "Go-Go Sox" stole far more bases than any other MLB team but fell to the Dodgers in the World Series. Over the next several decades, the Sox continued to be one of the league's stronger teams, but they seemed to specialize in the bridesmaid's role, finishing second 13 times between 1963 and 2004.

In that last year, the Sox hired Ozzie Guillen, their volatile, opinionated former shortstop, as manager. Guillen connected strongly with the players, and in 2005 the White Sox finally won their first World Series since Shoeless Joe roamed left field.

Jermaine Dye got three base hits in Game 4 of the 2005 Fall Classic, earning Series MVP honors while helping the White Sox win the crown for the first time in 88 years.

THE TRIBUNE ALWAYS MAKES A HIT WITH ITS SPORTING

THE HITLESS WONDERS

The 1906 intra-city World Series pitted the Cubs against the White Sox's team of "Hitless Wonders." Despite being the Series underdog, the Pale Hose managed to upset their cross-town rivals.

Most people thought Hugh Fullerton was crazy. In 1906, just before Chicago's first intra-city World Series between the Cubs and White Sox, the *Chicago Tribune* sportswriter went against the stream by picking the Sox to win. Not only that, but he specified that they would win Games 1, 3, 5 and 6.

No World Series before or since has featured a bigger mismatch. The Cubs, behind the pitching of Mordecai "Three Finger" Brown and the superb infield defense of Joe Tinker, Johnny Evers and Frank Chance, went 116-36 en route to the NL pennant, which remains the best regular-season record of all time. The White Sox, on the other hand, were dubbed "Hitless Wonders" for their offensive futility. The Sox had found ways to score runs without getting hits. Their 226 sacrifices topped the next-highest AL total by 35, and their 453 walks led the league by nearly 70.

The Cubs had won 55 of their final 65 games and featured the poetic double-play combination of Tinker to Evers to Chance. Comparatively, although the White Sox triumphed in 93 games, they owned a league-worst .230 batting average, and their double-play combo — George Davis to Frank Isbell to Jiggs Donahue — was hardly the well-oiled machine of their counterparts on the North Side.

Sox player-manager Fielder Jones admitted that his top pitcher, Ed Walsh, was "certainly not as good" as the Cubs' Brown, and avoided a Game 1 showdown of aces by offering lefty Nick Altrock as a sacrifice. Altrock, though, beat Brown, 2-1, and after the Sox lost the next game, Walsh pitched a two-hit shutout in Game 3. The upstart Sox went on to take the Series, winning exactly the games Fullerton had predicted, including an 8-3 pounding of Brown in Game 6. "The battle was a hot, furious one," wrote George Rice in the Spalding Guide. "Nothing seemed to turn out as had been predicted." Except for Fullerton's prediction, that is.

Neither team hit much during the Series: The Sox batted .198, the Cubs hit .196 and neither team homered. The player-managers, Jones and Chance, combined to go 7 for 42 without driving in a run. It was a Series tailor-made for those preferring pitching duels to a barrage of slap-hits, and it established the "Hitless Wonders" nickname as one fully earned — by both teams.

THE BIG HURT

On May 27, 1968 — the day after Dodgers righty Don Drysdale ran his historic scoreless streak to 36 innings — two boys were born who would cause nightmares for innumerable future pitchers. In Boston, Jan Bagwell gave birth to Jeff, who would be the 1994 NL MVP. And about 1,200 miles south in Columbus, Ga., Charlie Mae Thomas gave birth to Frank, the other circuit's 1994

Frank "The Big Hurt" Thomas, the owner of the 1993 and '94 AL MVP Awards, remains one of the most fearsome sluggers in White Sox history.

Most Valuable Player. Between these two, 970 future home runs were birthed on one day — not exactly a red-letter moment for pitchers.

A tight end on Auburn University's football team, Frank Thomas was one of the largest men ever to play in the Majors — a fact reflected in the nickname, "The Big Hurt," given by White Sox announcer Hawk Harrelson. The handle was a good one — all that the hulking Thomas did from the start was smash opposing hurlers into submission. Brought up to the Bigs as a highly touted prospect in the middle of the 1990 pennant race, Thomas batted .330 and slugged .529 in half a season. He soon put even those numbers to shame, leading the AL in walks, OBP and OPS four times each from 1991–97. In 1994, Thomas's stat line was simply mind-blowing: a .487 on-base percentage and an earth-shattering 1.217 OPS, a single-season mark that at the time had only been reached by Babe Ruth, Ted Williams, Lou Gehrig, Rogers Hornsby and Jimmie Foxx.

By the time his career ended in 2008, Thomas had put up lifetime numbers worthy of those greats: a .301 average, 521 homers and a .419 OBP. Although he was injured and unable to play in the postseason, Thomas picked up his long-awaited World Series ring when the Sox won it all in 2005. "Frank's a legend," teammate Willie Harris told ESPN.com. "He's Mr. White Sox."

GROUNDBREAKING

Saturnino Orestes Armas Minoso Arrieta, better known as "Minnie," was named to nine All-Star teams, won three Gold Gloves in the outfield and held the unofficial title of White Sox goodwill ambassador during a stellar career that spanned five decades. "My parents did

The franchise's first black player, Minoso was a nine-time All-Star with the White Sox.

White Sox Hall of Famers	
LUIS APARICIO	The shortstop stole 318 bases with Chicago — second on the franchise list.
LUKE APPLING	A career White Sox player, he won two batting titles (1936 and '43).
EDDIE COLLINS	Over the course of 25 seasons, he racked up 3,315 career hits.
RED FABER	As a 26-year-old, he won 24 games in his second Big League season.
NELLIE FOX	The second baseman won three Gold Gloves and the 1959 MVP Award.
TED LYONS	At age 41, he topped the AL with a 2.10 ERA in 1942.
RAY SCHALK	As a backstop, he caught a Major League record four no-hitters (a mark later matched by Jason Varitek).
ED WALSH	Big Ed's 40 wins in 1908 are a franchise record.

In his first Big League campaign, Jenks was an integral part of the White Sox victory in the 2005 World Series against the Houston Astros. The rookie notched four saves in that year's postseason.

not have the financial resources to send me to college or the polytechnic institute," said the club's first black player, "so I plowed the fields, planted, fertilized, weeded and cut the sugar cane. I'd sooner have had a bat in my hand than a farm implement."

Minoso's hitting prowess produced a .298 career batting average and 186 home runs with 1,136 runs and 205 stolen bases. The Cuba native debuted in 1949 with Cleveland and joined the White Sox in 1951. Minoso stayed in Chicago through the 1957 season, then returned in 1960 after two more seasons in Cleveland. He went to St. Louis in 1962 and then Washington in 1963, before re-joining the White Sox for 30 games in 1964. After a 12-year hiatus, Minoso returned to Chicago again in 1976, going 1 for 8 in three games. Four years later, he gave it one more shot at the age of 57, playing in two games and recording no hits in two at-bats.

WORTH THE WAIT

If, in April 2005, you made a list of the pitchers most likely to be standing victoriously on the mound at the end of that year's World Series, White Sox relief pitcher Bobby Jenks would have been about No. 1,000 on the list. Maybe 2,000. To that point in his career, Jenks was the real-life embodiment of *Bull Durham*'s Nuke LaLoosh.

Jenks had been dazzling scouts in the Angels' farm system with pitches clocked as fast as 102 mph since the club selected him in the fifth round of the 2000 draft. Trouble was, that was also the speed at which he lived his life. There was no party Jenks wasn't the life of and no rule he wouldn't break. In high school, he was academically ineligible for three of his four seasons. In December 2004, the Angels, tired of the headaches, let the White Sox claim him off waivers.

To his credit, Jenks used that as a wake-up call. "I got tired of going back to Double-A," he said. He blazed quickly through the Minor Leagues the next season and was the Sox's regular closer by mid-September. From the first save he recorded on Aug. 25 through the end of the regular season, Jenks went 6 for 8 in save opportunities while striking out 26 batters in 21 innings pitched during that stretch.

He earned a pair of saves in tight ALDS games against the Red Sox, and then dominated the Astros in the 2005 World Series. Jenks saved two of the four games and pitched two scoreless innings in another. He also provided one of the Series' few comical moments when Sox Manager Ozzie Guillen, with two right-handers warming up simultaneously, used exaggerated arm signals to indicate he wanted the big-bellied, tall guy. The 6-foot-3, 270-pound Jenks came jogging in from the bullpen — which, during the 2005 playoffs, was a sure sign that the game was in the books.

World Series champions for the third time in club history, the White Sox enjoyed a ticker-tape parade through the Windy City in 2005.

CINCINNATI REDS

FOR THE FIRST 37 YEARS THAT the World Series existed, the Cincinnati Reds won just one Fall Classic, but the franchise broke through with another world title in 1940. The next National League pennant didn't come until 1961, when a number of players had career years and plucky Cincinnati eked out a surprising first-place finish.

The franchise's true coming of age, though, can be traced to April 8, 1963, the day that Peter Edward Rose made his Major League debut. The pesky and versatile Rose became an All-Star starter at five different positions, enabling skipper Sparky Anderson to deploy the rest of his roster with maximum efficiency. And what a roster it was. Rose was joined by fellow MVP winners Johnny Bench, who revolutionized the catching position both offensively and defensively, and Joe Morgan, whose 1976 campaign was probably the greatest ever by a second baseman. With the nucleus of Rose, Bench and Morgan, the Big Red Machine breezed to back-to-back championships in 1975 and '76.

Controversy flared during the 1989 season when Rose, just four years removed from breaking Ty Cobb's career hits record, accepted a lifetime ban for betting on baseball while managing the club. The Reds quickly propelled themselves out of Rose's shadow, though. In 1990, Hall of Fame shortstop Barry Larkin, along with pitcher Jose Rijo and the famed "Nasty Boys" bullpen, led Cincinnati to one of the most shocking upsets in World Series annals by sweeping mighty Oakland. It was a much-needed salve for one of the game's most storied franchises.

Larkin again led the team to the postseason in 1995, when he won his first and only MVP Award, but the Reds bowed out in the NLCS. It took another 15 years for the club to return to the playoffs, when they won the NL Central behind the bat of first baseman Joey Votto, who took home the 2010 MVP Award following the season.

There was no more menacing National
League team during the 1970s than the
Big Red Machine, which featured (from left)
Rose, Morgan and Bench. Cincinnati won
two World Series in the decade.

THE BIG RED MACHINE

The Reds had enjoyed a great deal of regular-season success from the early to mid-1970s, and in 1975, that great group known as the Big Red Machine won a World Series. With Johnny Bench behind the plate, Tony Perez at first, Joe Morgan at second, Davey Concepcion at shortstop, Pete Rose at third and an outfield of George Foster, Cesar Geronimo and Ken Griffey, it wasn't a huge surprise when the Reds outlasted the Red Sox in a riveting Fall Classic.

Reflecting on the Series, Morgan has fond memories. "Look, everyone who played in the '75 Series has to consider it the greatest baseball experience of their lives, and I'm no exception," he says.

Still, the former second baseman has equally fond memories of the 1976 Series, another Cincinnati triumph. That season, the team led in the NL West wire-to-wire and finished 10 games clear of the competition, at 102-60. The Reds then rolled through the playoffs, first sweeping Philadelphia, then making it eight consecutive postseason wins with their sweep of the Yankees.

The Machine's offense was remarkable, leading the Majors in runs scored, average and home runs. Bench alone batted .533 in the Series to take MVP honors. Rose, a career .321 hitter in the playoffs, had nine hits in 30 trips in 1976 after hitting .323 during the regular campaign, his 14th of 24 seasons in the Majors.

"The team had it all going," said Morgan. "We had power, speed, great defense, a really good bullpen and solid starters. And those teams we beat in the postseason were very good … But we didn't lose a game to either of them."

NO FEAR

Instead of getting bashed by the Bash Brothers, the Cincinnati Reds did the slugging in the 1990 Fall Classic. Taking the field against a heavily favored A's juggernaut led by Jose Canseco and Mark McGwire, the Reds didn't roll over. Instead, their remarkable bullpen held Oakland's fearsome sluggers in check, propelling the Reds to a four-game sweep.

The Athletics, appearing in their third straight Fall Classic, were supposed to be riding the wave of a dynasty. Oakland's talented outfielders — Dave Henderson in center, flanked by Rickey Henderson in left and Canseco in right — averaged 28 homers apiece, and McGwire clubbed 39 as the team romped to a 103-59 regular-season record. But led by ace starting pitcher Jose Rijo, Cincinnati hurlers limited the Athletics to just eight runs in four World Series games and the amazing "Nasty Boys" in the bullpen — Rob Dibble, Randy Myers and Norm Charlton — hurled a combined 8.2 scoreless innings.

Mighty Oakland batted an unmighty .207 in the Series as McGwire and Canseco combined for one home run in 26 at-bats. "This is what you dream of — beating the defending champs, a supposed dynasty," Reds third baseman Chris Sabo said. "We beat 'em fair and square … we're the best now, and that's a fact."

Rijo twirled seven shutout innings to win Game 1 of the 1990 Fall Classic, then gave up just one run in Game 4.

HIT MAN

The all-time hits king, Rose finished with a .303 career batting average and, more impressively, 4,256 career hits in 24 seasons.

Although Reds player-manager Pete Rose left Cincinnati prior to the 1979 season and signed with the Philadelphia Phillies, he returned for the final two years of his playing career in 1985 and '86. By that time, thanks to years spent as a Big League hitting machine (including three NL batting titles), Rose had Ty Cobb's all-time hits record of 4,191 in his sights.

He would play just 119 games in '85, but it was enough to push him ahead of the Detroit Tigers' Hall of Famer. His record-setting base knock came against San Diego's Eric Show on Sept. 11. After that hit, as the crowd flooded the ever-hustling Rose with cheers, he lifted first base above his head — the culmination of decades of sharp swings and scraped knees. Rose finished with 4,256 hits to his name.

MLB's Top Hitsmen

	YRS	AVG	H	1B	2B	3B	HR
PETE ROSE	24	.303	4,256	3,125	746	135	160
TY COBB	24	.367	4,191	3,054	723	297	117
HANK AARON	23	.305	3,771	2,294	624	98	755
STAN MUSIAL	22	.331	3,630	2,253	725	177	475
TRIS SPEAKER	22	.345	3,514	2,383	792	222	117

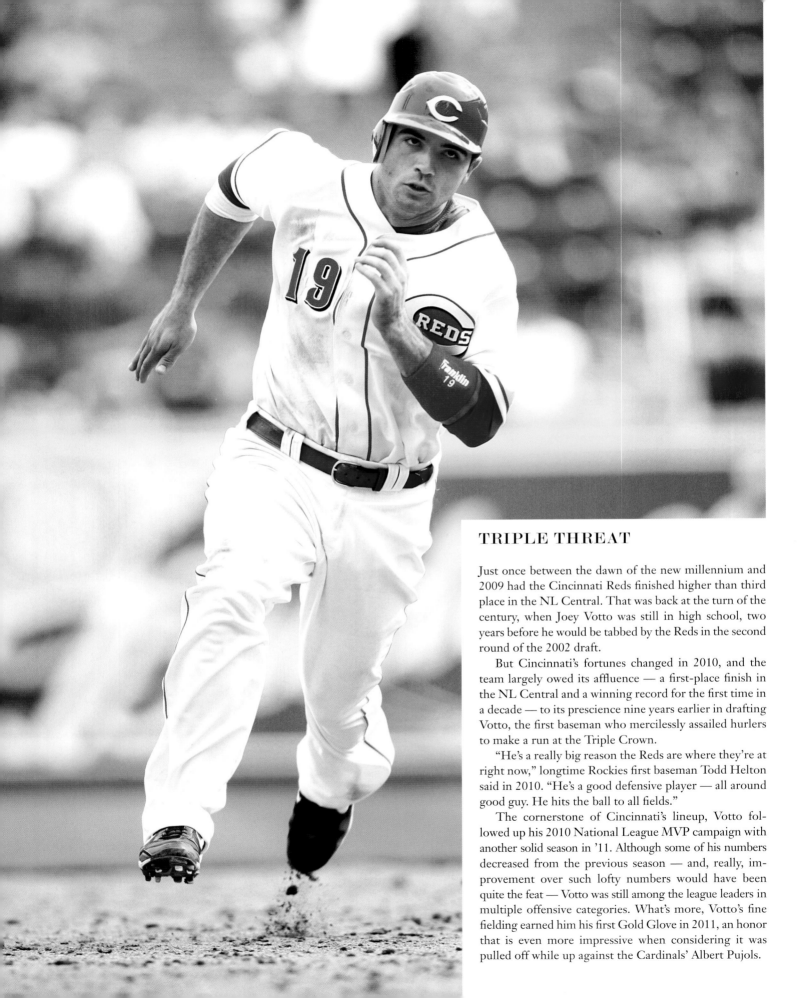

TRIPLE THREAT

Just once between the dawn of the new millennium and 2009 had the Cincinnati Reds finished higher than third place in the NL Central. That was back at the turn of the century, when Joey Votto was still in high school, two years before he would be tabbed by the Reds in the second round of the 2002 draft.

But Cincinnati's fortunes changed in 2010, and the team largely owed its affluence — a first-place finish in the NL Central and a winning record for the first time in a decade — to its prescience nine years earlier in drafting Votto, the first baseman who mercilessly assailed hurlers to make a run at the Triple Crown.

"He's a really big reason the Reds are where they're at right now," longtime Rockies first baseman Todd Helton said in 2010. "He's a good defensive player — all around good guy. He hits the ball to all fields."

The cornerstone of Cincinnati's lineup, Votto followed up his 2010 National League MVP campaign with another solid season in '11. Although some of his numbers decreased from the previous season — and, really, improvement over such lofty numbers would have been quite the feat — Votto was still among the league leaders in multiple offensive categories. What's more, Votto's fine fielding earned him his first Gold Glove in 2011, an honor that is even more impressive when considering it was pulled off while up against the Cardinals' Albert Pujols.

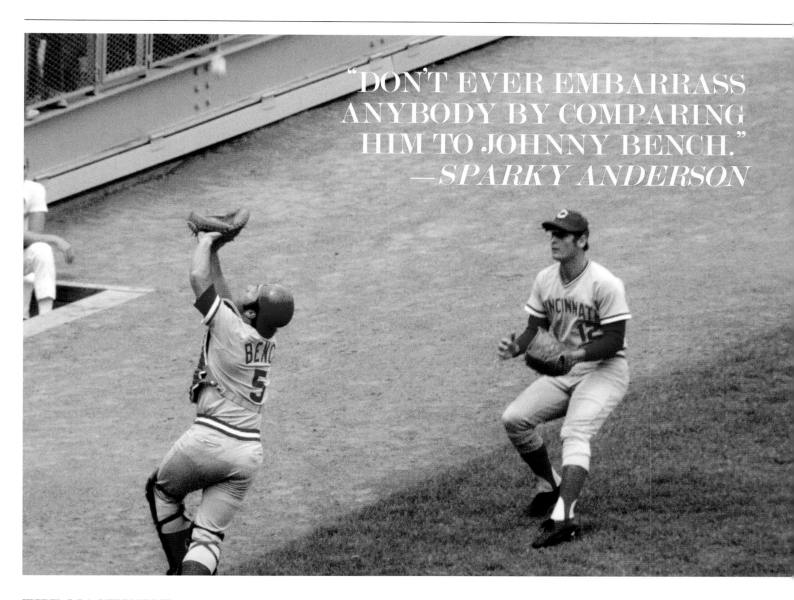

"DON'T EVER EMBARRASS ANYBODY BY COMPARING HIM TO JOHNNY BENCH."
—*SPARKY ANDERSON*

THE MACHINIST

The most famous quote uttered about Johnny Bench came from the flappable lips of his manager, Sparky Anderson, after the 1976 World Series: "Don't ever embarrass anybody by comparing him to Johnny Bench," he said.

When catching is discussed, Bench is the gold standard. The superlative numbers are endless: 14 All-Star nods, 10 Gold Gloves, Rookie of the Year (first catcher ever to win it), two MVP Awards and a World Series MVP Award.

There were 35 players drafted ahead of him in 1965, but he was a trailblazer on the field. (Among other feats, he became the first catcher to wear a batting helmet behind the plate, something he started in his first year in the Minors.)

During Spring Training 1968, before Bench's first full season, he was catching veteran righty Jim Maloney, whose fastball had lost velocity after injuries. Maloney was in love with that pitch and insisted on throwing it, ignoring Bench's repeated signs for breaking balls. Finally, after Maloney shook off one too many calls for a breaking ball — preferring to throw his lukewarm heater — Bench removed his glove as Maloney released the pitch. Bench caught the throw barehanded. Point made.

Ultimately, bad knees shortened Bench's career and forced him to finish it playing the infield. The Reds held "Johnny Bench Night" on Sept. 17, 1983, and in true Bench fashion, he hit a home run, the 389th and last of his Hall of Fame career.

Votto (opposite) made a run at the Triple Crown in 2010. Bench's (above, left) accolades include 14 All-Star nods, 10 Gold Gloves and two NL MVP Awards.

CLEVELAND INDIANS

THE CLEVELAND INDIANS HAVE always been a team of big pendulum swings. Although they've had their share of extended periods without a pennant — prompting the makers of *Major League* to select the Tribe as the film's struggling baseball franchise — they've also had several long stretches of dominance, such as the offensive powerhouse that rose to prominence in the mid-to-late '90s and reached two World Series.

In 1936, Cleveland rookie Bob Feller became the first pitcher to record a game with the same number of strikeouts as his age — 17. In June of his second Big League season, the young sensation returned home to Van Meter, Iowa, for his high school graduation, which was broadcast nationwide on NBC Radio. Feller pitched on pennant-winning Indians teams in 1948 and '54, the latter of which won a then-AL-record 111 games but got swept in the World Series.

During the ensuing decades, the Indians found it difficult to get over the hump, with a prime example of their fate being the ill-advised 1960 trade of slugger Rocky Colavito, which sent a second-place team tumbling into fourth. Not until the 1990s did Cleveland finally put together a consistent winner, capturing five consecutive AL Central titles with a mixture of homegrown talent (Albert Belle, Jim Thome) and savvy trade acquisitions (Kenny Lofton, Omar Vizquel). These mighty offensive teams won the 1995 and '97 pennants, coming just two out from winning it all in the ninth inning of Game 7 of the '97 Fall Classic.

At just 17 years old and in the midst of his first Big League campaign, Feller already looked like a future Hall of Famer. He recorded 17 K's in one game against the A's and, during his second season, returned home to take part in his high school graduation ceremony.

livestock. Few days went by without Feller throwing a baseball around with his father or throwing against the side of the family barn, either.

In 1936, Feller tried out for the Cleveland Indians in an exhibition game against the St. Louis Cardinals and whiffed eight of the nine Big Leaguers he faced. The 17-year-old would compile 76 strikeouts in 62 Big League innings before the year was through. Two years later — despite being just 19 — he tied Mel Harder for the club lead with 17 wins while also making his first All-Star team.

PIONEER

Larry Doby is best known as the second African-American baseball player to make his way to the Major Leagues and the first to play in the American League. It's not inaccurate — it's just not completely fair, because Larry Doby was so much more.

A career .283 hitter, Doby twice led the league in homers, in 1952 becoming the first black player to accomplish the feat. He was named to all seven All-Star Games between 1949 and 1955 and played in two World Series — helping lead the Indians to the title in 1948. In that Series, Doby led the team with a .318 batting average, and hit a game-winning home run off the Braves' Johnny Sain in Game 4. Despite knowing that any strikeout, any fielding error, any double play he grounded into could sidetrack not only his progression, but also that of aspiring black players everywhere, he never cowered.

Like Jackie Robinson, Doby witnessed the wicked underbelly of America's facility with labels. At least publicly, Doby chose to savor the good; Hall of Famer Joe Morgan remembered that he would never identify the players who had mistreated him, allowing himself only to point out those, such as teammates Joe Gordon and Steve Gromek, who had stood up and embraced him. And he always saved a special place for Bill Veeck, the legendary owner who opened himself up to criticism and rage when he signed Doby away from Newark of the Negro Leagues.

Regardless of race, today's players face many pressures that could never have been imagined half a century ago. But none have to deal with the hardship of representing their entire race in one at-bat, of knowing that their visibility alone made them a hated scapegoat. It's a pressure that few could have handled, but like Robinson before him, Doby was the perfect man to bare such a burden. And the world is a better place for it.

RAPID RISE TO GREATNESS

Had he not volunteered to serve in the United States Navy during World War II — missing out on nearly four full Major League seasons — Bob Feller would have almost definitely reached 300 wins. Instead, the career Cleveland Indians pitcher, nicknamed "Rapid Robert" for his whistling fastball, retired with 266. At his induction ceremony into Cooperstown in 1962, the first-ballot Hall of Famer said that he had no regrets about enlisting. And later in life, he put up a noble fight to get other deserving ballplayers whose careers were shortened by a call to duty into the Hall of Fame.

According to an army machine usually reserved for measuring the speed of artillery shells, Feller's famous fastball was speeding home at 98.6 mph upon his return from war, showing that he didn't develop much — if any — rust in his three-plus seasons away from the game. That same year, he fanned a career-high 348 batters, one of seven seasons in which he paced the AL and the only one in which he struck out more than 300 hitters.

Feller was known to credit his childhood chores for his incredible velocity. Born on an Iowa farm, he built strength just working through his daily regimen with the

Nicknamed "Rapid Robert," Feller was known for his velocity. The Iowa farmboy also had a penchant for racking up plenty of strikeouts.

 Rock & Roll

74 **PITCHES** thrown by Addie Joss during his perfect game for the Indians on Oct. 2, 1908. He would win 160 games in nine years with the team.

455 **STRAIGHT SELLOUTS** recorded by the Indians at home, then a Big League record. The streak ended in 2001 and was eventually overtaken in 2008 by the Boston Red Sox.

.283 **CAREER BATTING AVERAGE** recorded by Larry Doby. The first African-American to play in the American League, Doby faced great turmoil throughout his early days in the Majors. He debuted during the 1947 season and thrived over the course of his career.

111 **WINS** registered during the 1954 season, an American League record that stood for 44 years. The Indians were led on the field by sluggers Doby and Al Rosen, as well as an impressive pitching rotation.

97 **WINS** recorded by the 1999 Cleveland Indians on their way to a fifth straight AL Central crown. Right fielder Manny Ramirez led the way with 44 homers and 165 RBI.

3,000 **HITS** reached by Nap Lajoie on Sept. 27, 1914. He was the first in Cleveland history to reach the mark.

The first black player in the AL, Doby (right) shunned those who mistreated him and chose instead to embrace those who accepted him, like Gromek, who celebrated with Doby after the Tribe's 1948 World Series Game 4 win.

THE INDIANS HAVE
BEEN A TEAM OF
PENDULUM SWINGS.
THEY'VE HAD PERIODS
WITHOUT A PENNANT,
BUT THEY'VE ALSO
HAD LONG STRETCHES
OF DOMINANCE.

CHILD'S PLAY

Lou Boudreau majored in physical education at the University of Illinois and played for the Illini basketball team before trying to break into pro baseball. At the tender age of 24, he mailed a letter to Cleveland Indians Owner Alva Bradley suggesting the attributes that qualified him to be the team's player-manager.

"I realize it was a very brash thing to do," he said more than 50 years later. But Bradley was sufficiently intrigued to call Boudreau to a meeting with club directors. Even more shocking than the invitation, the Indians actually picked Boudreau over two other candidates to succeed Roger Peckinpaugh as the team's manager in 1942.

The press immediately dubbed Boudreau the "Boy Manager," but nobody cut him any slack because of his youth. The overall reaction was skeptical, to put it mildly.

"Great! The Indians get a Baby Snooks for a manager and ruin the best shortstop in baseball," wrote one Cleveland reporter.

With experience and time, Boudreau proved adept at multi-tasking. In 1948, he won the American League MVP Award and managed the Indians to 97 victories, an AL pennant and a World Series victory over the Boston Braves. At 30 years old, he had reached the pinnacle of both of his endeavors, in more ways than one.

SPEAKER OF THE HOUSE

Although his place among baseball's all-time greats is well established, Tris Speaker would probably be even more legendary had he not suffered the misfortune of spending most of his career in direct competition with Ty Cobb, who always seemed to edge out Speaker in the box score. In 1912, when Speaker batted .383, Cobb hit .409. Ten years later, Speaker averaged .378, only to see Cobb post a .401 mark.

But Speaker was notably better than his rival at two things: playing defense and winning. Over Speaker's 20 full seasons in the Majors, he played for 17 winning teams and bagged three world championships.

Boudreau (opposite) may have played decades after Speaker (left), but both were among the best players of their respective eras. Boudreau was the 1948 AL MVP, while Speaker holds the MLB record for doubles.

Of course, having an offensive output slightly less than Cobb's is nothing to be ashamed of. Speaker's lifetime average of .345 still ranks sixth all-time, one point ahead of Ted Williams' mark, and his 436 career stolen bases are evidence of the heartache he caused as a base runner. "The Grey Eagle" — so named for his prematurely white hair — was also the first left-handed hitter to become adept at smacking opposite-field doubles off Fenway Park's famed left-field wall. Speaker led the AL in two-baggers eight times. Even after the Red Sox traded him to Cleveland in 1916, Speaker continued pounding out two-base hits, leading the Majors in doubles every year from 1920–23. His lifetime total of 792 doubles remains the all-time MLB record, and his 3,514 hits still rank second in AL annals behind, you guessed it, Cobb.

But while Speaker always seemed to be chasing Cobb, legendary sportswriter Grantland Rice preferred to compare Speaker to another .400 hitter of the era — Nap Lajoie — for his grace. "Neither wasted a motion or gave you any sign of extra effort," Rice wrote of Speaker and Lajoie. "They had the same elements that made a Bobby Jones or the Four Horsemen of Notre Dame — the smoothness of a summer wind."

Lou Boudreau's career stats as a player and manager

	Seasons	Games	AB	AVG	OBP	HR	RBI	SB	R
PLAYER	15	1,646	6,029	.295	.380	68	789	51	861

	Seasons	Games	Wins	Losses	W-L Pct.	Pennants		WS Titles
MANAGER	16	2,404	1,162	1,224	.487	1		1

COLORADO ROCKIES

WHEN BIG LEAGUE BASEBALL finally arrived in Colorado in 1993, fans came to Mile High Stadium in unprecedented numbers to watch live, many of them for the first time. The expansion Rockies finished 67-95 in that debut year, but it didn't deter the 4.48 million fans who helped obliterate MLB's single-season attendance record.

With veteran hitters like Andres Galarraga, Larry Walker, Dante Bichette and Ellis Burks discovering that their bats worked much better in Denver than anywhere else, the Rockies made the playoffs in 1995, just their third season. But they nonetheless confronted perhaps the most perplexing challenge any front office has ever faced: How do you build a winning baseball team at a high altitude, where the game is so different? They tried speed and defense; they tried burly sluggers; they tried free-agent pitchers. They even tried to deaden baseballs by storing them in a humidor. For a decade nothing really worked, until the Rockies stumbled upon the seemingly obvious: building the team from the ground up, using the farm system. All you needed to trump altitude, it turned out, was talent.

In 2007, a Rockies club featuring homegrown superstars Todd Helton, Matt Holliday and Troy Tulowitzki found itself mired in fourth place on Sept. 16. For the next month, though, under lose-and-the-season-is-over pressure, Colorado performed as well as any team has ever played. By the time the dust settled, the Rockies had won 21 of 22 games and swept through both the NLDS and NLCS before falling in the World Series. The Rockies nabbed another Wild Card berth in 2009 while continuing to churn out the promising young players for which their farm system has become known.

Holliday and the rest of the never-say-die '07 Rockies tore through the late season, winning 21 of 22 games to earn the club's first National League pennant.

ROCK-TOBER

After a grueling 162-game season in 2007, the Rockies still were not ready to stop playing baseball. In fact, they were just getting started. By winning 13 of their last 14 games during the regular season, including a prophetic series win over the Arizona Diamondbacks in the 2007 regular season's final weekend, the Rockies forced a one-game playoff against the San Diego Padres with the National League Wild Card hanging in the balance. Before a raucous Coors Field crowd, the surging Rockies outlasted their NL West rivals, 9-8, when Matt Holliday's head-first, chin-bloodying slide into home plate scored the winning run in the bottom of the 13th inning. In just a few weeks, Colorado had gone from an also-ran in the oft-overlooked NL West to the hottest and most feared team in the country.

"I've never been a part of anything like this," said Manager Clint Hurdle, speaking about his club's dash to October. The same was true for his players — whether slick-fielding shortstop and Rookie of the Year candidate Troy Tulowitzki, NL batting champ and NLCS MVP Holliday or the club's all-time leader in almost every offensive category, Todd Helton — who had just six postseason appearances among them prior to '07. Still, nary a mental mistake nor missed opportunity occurred in either of the first two rounds of the playoffs as the Rockies swept the Phillies and the D-backs. With a relentless approach at the plate and a pitching staff led by 17-game winner Jeff Francis, the Rockies seemingly got better in every way as the wins piled up and the calendar got deeper into October.

The Rockies' unprecedented streak — they won 21 of 22 games leading up to the World Series — was no fluke. The team played historically good defense — its fielding percentage entering the playoffs (.98925) was the best regular-season mark in history. With Kazuo Matsui and Tulowitzki providing a reliable and energetic double-play combination up the middle and Willy Taveras making run-saving catches in center field (like the one he

snagged in Game 2 of the NLCS against the D-backs), opponents had a hard time following the old adage of "hit 'em where they ain't," because the Rockies seemed to be absolutely everywhere.

SKY WALKER

At 31 years old, Rockies outfielder Larry Walker capped off an historic 1997 campaign that compared favorably among the finest in league history. Walker became the first Rockie and native-born Canadian to win the National League's MVP Award, and he accomplished the feat hands down, receiving 22 of 28 possible first-place votes and 359 total points — 96 more than his closest competitor.

The sweet-swinger from Maple Ridge, British Columbia, came within four hits and 10 RBI of winning the only Triple Crown since 1967. Walker put his 6-foot-3 inch, 235-pound frame to excellent use, leading the league with 49 home runs, ranking second with a .366 batting average and finishing third in RBI with 130. He also topped the league with an astronomical .720 slugging percentage — fifth highest in NL history — and became one of just 14 players in Major League history to record more than 400 total bases in a season. For good measure, he received the league's Silver Slugger Award for offensive production at the position.

The passion and intensity he put toward achieving excellence in baseball were born on the frozen ponds and ice rinks north of the U.S. border where, not surprisingly, he grew up playing hockey.

"I fought a couple times as a goalie, I whacked people on the legs with my stick when they came in the crease," he said during his playing days. "I guess in a similar way, I'd run into a wall to try to catch a fly ball or I'd try to knock the shortstop into left field to break up a double play. I'm not afraid to go into the corners. There's a mental toughness in hockey that I tried to take into baseball."

To validate the '07 club's amazing run, Holliday's slide home (above) secured a playoff berth. Seven wins later, Helton secured the putout (opposite, left) to send Colorado to the Fall Classic.

 Mile High-lights

31 **BATTERS** faced by Rockies ace Ubaldo Jimenez during his no-hitter against the Atlanta Braves on April 17, 2010. It was the first no-hitter in franchise history, dating back to the club's first season in 1993.

14 **INNINGS** into Coors Field's first-ever game, on April 26, 1995, that Dante Bichette hit a walk-off homer to win an 11-9 slugfest that would become common in Denver's thin air.

4,483,350 **FANS** came out to watch the Rockies play home games in the team's inaugural 1993 season at the Denver Broncos' Mile High Stadium.

32 **STEALS** and 40 home runs put up by outfielder Ellis Burks in 1996, making him the first player in Rockies history to join the elite 30/30 club. Bichette joined Burks the next day.

.340 **BATTING AVERAGE** posted by Matt Holliday in 2007 to lead the NL. Holliday also raked 50 doubles, drove in a league-best 137 runs and ripped 36 home runs.

.98925 **FIELDING PERCENTAGE** recorded by the Rockies in the 2007 regular season, good for the best team mark in Big League history.

Walker (above, right) led the NL with a mammoth .720 slugging percentage and took home MVP honors in 1997. He also possessed a cannon of an arm in right field.

The city's thin air and its effect on traveling baseballs grabbed headlines, but Coors Field also stands out as one of the most scenic venues in the Major Leagues thanks to a beautiful ballpark and fantastic surroundings.

MILE ABOVE THE REST

No element has played a more significant role in the evolution of Coors Field than the high altitude of Denver. Aside from being accompanied by a scenic mountain view, the city's thin air has greatly affected the Rockies' history and success. While the stadium was being built, the franchise even installed a row of purple seats across the entire upper deck of Coors Field to mark the point exactly one mile above sea level.

The Rockies played their first two seasons at Mile High Stadium, also home to the NFL's Denver Broncos, before Coors Field opened in 1995. The stadium became another in a sequence of parks designed during the '90s with a "retro" feel. Originally built to hold 43,000 spectators, the young Rockies' impressive attendance at Mile High prompted an increase in capacity at the new Coors Field to more than 50,000.

Because the stadium sits so high, a baseball travels 9 percent farther than it does at sea level. For example, a 400-foot homer in a sea-level park turns into a 440-foot shot in Denver. Therefore, players and fans alike have always kept a close eye on the offensive numbers produced at Coors Field. On occasion, even the validity of outstanding seasons by players like Rockies outfielder Larry Walker — who took home the 1997 NL MVP Award — have been greeted with a certain level of skepticism due to the hitter-friendly nature of his home ballpark.

BUILT FOR 43,000, THE ROCKIES' IMPRESSIVE ATTENDANCE AT MILE HIGH PROMPTED AN INCREASE IN CAPACITY AT COORS TO 50,000.

In spite of efforts to curtail the offensive explosion, balls still flew out of the yard at a record pace. The home-run hysteria reached a crisis point in 2001, when teams combined for an average of 3.31 homers at Coors Field per game for a season total of 268. An astounding 13.4 combined runs per game were recorded that year when the Rockies played at home. Colorado would finally remedy the situation by installing a humidor to regulate the atmosphere's effect on their baseballs.

DETROIT TIGERS

RATHER QUIETLY, THE DETROIT Tigers have ranked among baseball's most tradition-laden franchises over the past century. Fans of the Cubs, Dodgers or Cardinals might dispute this, but consider that among the 16 "original" Major League clubs, just one — the Tigers — has never relocated or changed its name. Even today, the team's road jersey, with its "Detroit" script, is nearly identical to the one Hank Greenberg wore when he hit his pennant-winning grand slam on the last day of the 1945 season.

The first great player in Tigers annals was "Wahoo Sam" Crawford, who combined power, speed and a rifle arm to become an early prototype of the five-tool player. Ty Cobb joined Crawford full time in 1907, and the Tigers immediately captured three straight pennants — albeit losing the World Series each time. Despite phenomenal seasons like 1911, when he batted .420 with 83 steals and 127 RBI, the fiery Cobb never again returned to the Fall Classic. Much to his chagrin, he played his final World Series game at age 22.

A generation later, Greenberg and Charlie Gehringer turned the Tigers into perennial contenders, helping the team win four pennants and two championship rings. The next Tigers team to win a championship surfaced in 1968, featuring steady veteran Al Kaline and 31-game winner Denny McLain. Detroit's fourth title came in 1984, when Manager Sparky Anderson's club grabbed first place on Opening Day and never let go, utterly dominating the AL before winning the World Series on a pair of Kirk Gibson homers. More than two decades later, rookie Justin Verlander — who would win a Cy Young and an MVP award in 2011 — led the Tigers to the AL pennant in 2006, and they remained contenders in the ensuing years, picking up players such as sluggers Miguel Cabrera (signed before the 2008 season) and Prince Fielder (2012).

The 1934 Tigers were one of several dominant Detroit clubs to reach the World Series. Although they didn't take home the hardware that year, many players from that team returned to capture the trophy in '35.

EYE OF THE TIGER

For generations of fans who never saw the Georgia Peach play, Ty Cobb's unparalleled achievements often have been overshadowed by the star's temperamental personality. Since his death in 1961, something approaching a new historical consensus has emerged. In Lawrence Ritter's classic book, *The Glory of their Times*, former teammate Sam Crawford depicted Cobb as an angry Southerner "still fighting the Civil War."

There are plenty of incidents in Cobb's life to bolster such assertions. Quick-tempered and violent, Cobb was also, like many Americans at the time, an unrepentant racist. But those now quick to judge Cobb as nothing more than brutal and self-centered would do best to take another look at this complex, fascinating figure.

Cobb made millions during his lifetime — mainly from investing in Coca-Cola — and he donated much of his wealth to philanthropic causes. He established the Ty Cobb Memorial Hospital in his hometown of Royston, Ga., which to this day provides the community with much-needed healthcare. He also established the Cobb Education Fund, which provides college scholarships to needy Georgia students.

After he retired, Cobb also dispensed advice to young players such as Joe DiMaggio. In 1935, when DiMaggio was still a Minor Leaguer with the San Francisco Seals and haggling with New York Yankees ownership over his salary, Cobb orchestrated the negotiations by dictating letters to Yankees management, which were then signed by the reserved DiMaggio. Fed up with the subterfuge and having caught on to Cobb's tricks, General Manager Ed Barrow sent a final contract to DiMaggio with a note attached, saying, "This is the limit. Don't waste another three-cent stamp. Just sign it. And tell Cobb to stop writing me letters."

Cobb studied the game as intensely as any man before or since. Perhaps the most aggressive base runner ever, he knew the pickoff moves of every pitcher in the league and the arm strength of every catcher, and he constantly probed defenses for any weakness that he could exploit. To White Sox Owner Charles Comiskey, Cobb was "the greatest player of all time," an intelligent foe who played "with his whole anatomy — his head, his arms, his hands, his legs, his feet."

A 1942 poll in which managers chose the greatest player of all time picked Cobb over Babe Ruth. Casey Stengel, who managed DiMaggio and Mickey Mantle, and played against Ruth, declared, "I never saw anyone like Ty Cobb. No one even close to him." Perhaps more than any other player in history, Cobb was respected and feared, loved and hated, often at the same time.

Cobb was feared for his persona but revered for his playing abilities, ranking as the greatest player of all time in a 1942 managerial poll.

BRINGING THE HEAT

It had been 20 years since a pitcher — the A's Dennis Eckersley in 1992 — won a Most Valuable Player Award when Justin Verlander made his case in 2011. Other than Pedro Martinez at the turn of the century, there hadn't been a pitcher since Eckersley more deserving to take home the hardware than the Tigers' right-hander.

"I think 'dominating' is such a fierce term, because 'dominating' used to just be a massive fastball," said catcher Kelly Shoppach. "You know, like Nolan Ryan–type stuff. "I don't think, in the current game today, there's a guy with that kind of fastball — except maybe Verlander."

Being named in an analogy with the Ryan Express is no small praise, but Verlander has certainly been up to the comparison thus far in his career. Becoming the fastest pitcher to reach 20 wins in a season since Curt Schilling in 2002, Verlander burst out of the gate in 2011 and never slowed down his pace. From his second career no-hitter in May, to a 14-strikeout showing against the Diamondbacks in June, to a stretch of nine consecutive starts with seven-plus innings of work and two earned runs or fewer allowed, Verlander proved to be the epitome of "dominant" in 2011.

"He has three-plus pitches that he throws at any given time," said Braves center fielder Michael Bourn. "And he can still throw 100 mph in the eighth inning. That's pretty good."

Good is an understatement. Featuring that fastball, a sharp curve and a change-up that — at 86 mph — turns his opponents into corkscrews, he would indeed take home both the 2011 MVP Award and Cy Young Award.

Verlander's sheer dominance on the mound earned him the AL MVP Award in 2011.

The Tigers have quietly become one of MLB's most tradition-rich clubs. After playing for decades in Tiger Stadium, in 2000 the club moved to Comerica Park, which has a retro feel and celebrates Tigers history.

TIGER TRACKS

To this day in Detroit, the 1968 Tigers — more than any other championship team in any sport in any time — remain synonymous with success.

In February 1968, the club reported to Spring Training confident about winning it all. "Inwardly, we were determined to prove that we were the best team in the American League," pitcher Mickey Lolich acknowledged. And the '68 season indeed turned out to be the "Year of the Tiger."

Al Kaline, a Tigers fixture since 1954 and a future Hall of Famer, had waited his entire career for the chance to play in a World Series. But he had missed five weeks of the season with a broken hand and, in his absence, the outfield of Willie Horton in left, Mickey Stanley in center and Jim Northrup in right had played extremely well. Late in the season, knowing that light-hitting shortstop Ray Oyler was the weak link in the Tigers' attack, Manager Mayo Smith secretly summoned Stanley, who hadn't made an error in center field all year, and asked, "How would you like to play shortstop in the World Series? If you can play shortstop, I can put Kaline in the outfield and I think our ballclub would be better offensively than it's ever been," Smith explained.

"When do I start?" Stanley, a gifted all-around athlete, replied with a grin.

With Stanley at short, Kaline back in right and lefty Lolich upstaging teammate and 31-game winner Denny McLain with wins in Games 2, 5 and 7, the Tigers rallied from a 3-games-to-1 deficit against Bob Gibson's Cardinals. Fifty-thousand people packed the runway at Detroit's Metro Airport to welcome their team home, forcing the Tigers' flight to divert to Willow Run airport near Ann Arbor, Mich., where 5,000 frenzied fans waited.

The win couldn't have come at a better time, with the memories of Detroit's 1967 race riot still vivid in people's memories. "I believe," Willie Horton later declared, "the '68 Tigers were put here by God to heal this city."

It would be 16 years before Detroit baseball fans would know such joy again. Like their predecessors in '35 and '68, the 1984 Tigers owned the city. They jumped out to a remarkable 35-5 start and set the pace in the American League East from Opening Day, attracting 2.7 million fans, a franchise record that would not be broken until 2007. Then they rolled over the Kansas City Royals and San Diego Padres in the postseason.

"Don't ever forget this moment," skipper Sparky Anderson told his club. "You did it all."

McLain (left) didn't fare as well as his teammate Lolich in the 1968 World Series, but he did contribute a win in Game 6. In 1984, Lance Parrish (right) came up big, homering in the decisive Game 5 to give the Tigers the '84 crown.

MR. TIGER

When he retired in 1974 at the age of 39, Al Kaline trailed just four Major Leaguers in games played — Hall of Famers Hank Aaron, Ty Cobb, Stan Musial and Willie Mays. He had won a World Series and a batting title, earned 10 Gold Gloves and 18 All-Star selections, and racked up 3,007 hits. A trip to Cooperstown lay ahead, and in 1980 the Tigers' legend became just the 10th player to gain election to the Hall of Fame in his first appearance on the ballot since the Hall's five-year wait rule was instituted in 1954.

During his 22-year career, spent entirely with Detroit, Kaline accumulated some hefty totals. But there's one number he became best known for; in fact, known *as*: "6," which he wore on his back for 21 of those seasons. Other players have had their uniform numbers retired and immortalized, but even then it remains just another tidbit of trivia for fans to memorize as proof of true devotion. With Kaline, it meant something more. He picked up other nicknames — "Mr. Tiger," "Mr. Perfection," "The Line" (a play on his name and his consistency) — but being known just by his number best described how he was on the field.

In the long run, Kaline fell short of several of these extremely high expectations: He never won another batting title (unlike Cobb, who claimed 12 altogether), and never hit more than 29 homers in a season. He reached 3,000 hits, but barely missed a few other milestones with 399 home runs and a .297 career average.

After collecting his 3,000th base knock in 1974, "The Line" came to an end — but only in terms of his playing career. Kaline would move into the Tigers' broadcast booth, later teach Kirk Gibson how to play the outfield and then, 50 years after taking home an AL batting title, begin to serve as a special assistant to Team President Dave Dombrowski in 2002.

Kaline, better known in Detroit simply as No. 6, was a career Tiger and first-ballot Hall of Famer who has been immortalized in Michigan.

 On the Prowl

958 RUNS scored by the 1934 team, setting a club record. With seven .300 hitters in the everyday lineup, Detroit was a dominant force.

0 RUNS allowed by left-hander Kenny Rogers during his three postseason starts for the Tigers in 2006. Rogers went 3-0 in the playoffs but the Tigers fell to the St. Louis Cardinals in the World Series.

20 YEARS OLD, Al Kaline's age in 1955 when he led the Junior Circuit with a .340 average. He was the youngest player in league history ever to win a batting crown.

17 SEASONS overseen by skipper Sparky Anderson between 1979 and 1995. The legendary manager led the team to the 1984 World Series championship and won more than 1,300 games.

183 RBI accumulated by Hank Greenberg in 1937 to lead the AL. Only Hack Wilson (191) and Lou Gehrig (184) have ever racked up more in a season.

9 RUNS, the deficit faced by the 1901 club in the final inning of their first game in the AL. The team rallied and won, 14-13, on a double by Frank "Pop" Dillon.

HOUSTON ASTROS

T
HE HOUSTON ASTROS WERE born in 1962 as the Colt .45s, a symbol of the bygone West, but before long they had a space-age nickname to go along with a futuristic new ballpark. Judge Roy Hofheinz, the team's larger-than-life owner, renamed the club the Astros in 1965, when he shook baseball to its core by opening the world's first domed stadium. At first the Astrodome sported real grass, but roof panels blocked out too much sunlight for the grass to flourish — so in 1966, Houston again upset baseball's traditionalist apple cart by installing a synthetic grass dubbed AstroTurf.

Technological innovations aside, the early Astros boasted some great players, too. Texas native and Hall of Famer Joe Morgan started his career as a Colt .45, but it was longer-tenured Astros like diminutive slugger Jimmy Wynn, precocious hurler Larry Dierker, and fan-favorite Jose Cruz who really captured Houstonians' hearts. In 1980, a tragic stroke ended the career of strikeout king J.R. Richard, but newly signed free agent Nolan Ryan picked up the slack, helping the franchise to its first-ever playoff berth that October.

But the greatest years in Astros history came from 1991–2005, when "Killer B's" Jeff Bagwell and Craig Biggio — and, starting in 1999, Lance Berkman — called Houston home. Bagwell, acquired from the Boston Red Sox as a Minor Leaguer for reliever Larry Andersen in what is considered one of baseball history's most lopsided trades, hit 449 home runs and won the 1994 NL MVP Award. Biggio, an All-Star at both catcher and second base, reached base 4,505 times in his career. Together, the pair carried Houston to 12 winning seasons in 15 years as teammates, including the club's first pennant in 2005. Perhaps even more impressively, both men played every game of their long careers with the Astros.

The 2005 Astros enjoyed a wild ride, including an NL Division Series clinch over Atlanta in an 18-inning Game 4 marathon.

HARD THROWERS IN HOUSTON
HAVE BEEN A CONSTANT SINCE
THE MAJOR LEAGUE FRANCHISE
WAS INTRODUCED IN 1962.

THREE HORSES

Hard throwers in Houston have been a constant since the Major League franchise was introduced in 1962, but Mike Scott, J.R. Richard and Nolan Ryan hold three distinctions among the glittering list of Astros pitchers: Scott and Richard are the only hurlers to start an All-Star Game for the Astros, and they were the first two right-handers in National League history to strike out 300 or more batters in a season. Ryan … well, you might recognize him as the game's all-time strikeout king.

The Astros' No. 1 draft pick in 1969, Richard tied an NL record in 1971 when he struck out 15 batters in his first Major League start. But a lack of control kept him from securing a full-time spot in the rotation until 1975. In 1979, Richard was the main reason the Astros came from nowhere to challenge Cincinnati for the NL West title until the final week of the season, and in 1980, Richard seemed headed toward another level before he said his arm felt "dead" in June. At the time, he was 10-4 with a 1.90 ERA and 119 strikeouts, leading the Senior Circuit in all three categories. Shortly after the All-Star Game, Richard said he felt nauseous on the mound and his arm still didn't feel right. He went on the disabled list July 16. On July 30, he suffered a stroke during a supervised workout at the Astrodome and underwent life-saving surgery that day. Just 30 years old at the time, Richard never pitched in the Majors again.

Although he was almost released by the Astros in 1984, Scott became the best pitcher in baseball in 1986. At the age of 31, he won the Cy Young Award, the first and only pitcher to claim that honor in an Astros uniform. Scott led the Majors with 306 strikeouts, 275.1 innings pitched and a 2.22 ERA. On Sept. 25, he became the first pitcher to throw a no-hitter in a pennant- or division-clinching game, beating San Francisco at the Astrodome, 2-0, to give Houston the NL West title.

Ryan, meanwhile, was the prototypical gunslinger. But as his career wore on, he developed breaking pitches and became much better at locating his offerings, which allowed him to morph into a more complete pitcher.

He pitched for 27 seasons, during which he threw a Big League–record seven no-hitters, including one with the Astros on Sept. 26, 1981, against the Los Angeles Dodgers. In that game, Ryan struck out 11 batters and walked three, shutting down a team featuring such stars as Davey Lopes, Dusty Baker, Steve Garvey and Pedro Guerrero. Ryan then went on to become the game's all-time strikeout leader by a wide margin and the first to cross 5,000, which he did with the Texas Rangers in 1989.

From left: Scott and Richard are the only Astros pitchers to start an All-Star Game. Ryan tossed a no-hitter for Houston in 1981.

92

THE KILLER B's

Jeff Bagwell and Craig Biggio played more than 2,000 games together, forming Houston's defiant answer to baseball's roster whirlwind. The two outlasted more than 150 teammates and stuck around after the NFL's Houston Oilers moved to Tennessee and the Astros left the Astrodome. They had different styles — Biggio a speedy on-base waterbug and Bagwell a mashing slugger — with different mentalities. "Bagwell just sort of shows up and does his job," their former manager, Larry Dierker, once said. "Biggio goes down in the runway breaking things."

During their time together in Houston, Bagwell drove in Biggio 372 times, more than any other tandem in the Majors in the 30 years before and including that stretch.

That means that from Bagwell's rookie year in 1991 through 2005, 24 percent of his RBI involved a Biggio run and the same percentage of Biggio's runs scored were a result of a Bagwell plate appearance.

"We made it work," Biggio said. "He would take pitches when I was stealing a lot more bases, early enough to let you do your thing out there and get into scoring position.

"We worked well together for our whole careers. It's not like we were two home run hitters. I wasn't a home run hitter and he was. For years, when I got on, I knew I was scoring. If I got on twice, I knew he was driving me in at least once, if not both times."

Unfortunately for every other team during the Killer B's era, they knew it, too.

Over the course of 15 seasons together, Bagwell (left) drove in Biggio more than any other tandem in 30 years.

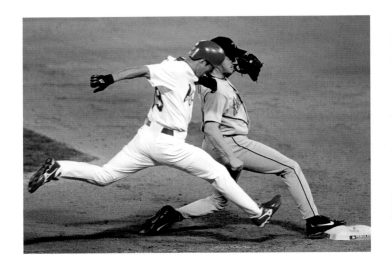

 Out of this World

3,056,139 **FANS** passed through the gates of the Astros' new stadium in 2000. Jeff Bagwell performed particularly well in front of the crowds, hitting a franchise-record 47 homers that season.

50,908 **FANS** in attendance at Houston's Astrodome on June 22, 1966, to watch Sandy Koufax and the Dodgers face their young home team. It was a team attendance record that stood for 32 years.

28 **DAYS** the Astros spent away from home during one road trip in 1992 due to the Republican Convention being in town. The team went 12-14 during that stretch.

16 **PICKS** into the first round of the 1997 draft, Houston nabbed Lance Berkman. In 12 seasons with the club, the on-base machine made five All-Star teams.

0 **HITS** allowed by Houston's Ken Johnson in nine innings on April 23, 1964. He still lost the game, 1-0, to Cincinnati, when two errors in the ninth led to a Reds run.

56 **STEALS** recorded by Cesar Cedeno in 1973, along with 25 homers. The dynamic young center fielder became the first player to record back-to-back 50-steal, 20-homer seasons.

SERIES-BOUND

Edging out the Philadelphia Phillies by a single game for the National League Wild Card in 2005, the Astros were determined to make the most of their spot in the postseason. The offensive core, with Jeff Bagwell and Craig Biggio, was mostly aging, and had relied on Lance Berkman and a breakout season from Morgan Ensberg. Pitching was the club's strength, and the Astros entered their Division Series matchup with the Atlanta Braves armed with Roy Oswalt, Andy Pettitte and Roger Clemens, plus the power relief arm of Brad Lidge.

Infielder Chris Burke memorably capped the Astros' four-game series victory over the Atlanta Braves in the NL Division Series by hitting a walk-off home run in the 18th inning against reliever Joey Devine. Game 4 featured 14 combined pitchers, including a relief appearance from Clemens that earned him the win.

The NLCS featured a showdown with the divisional rival St. Louis Cardinals, who were fresh off being swept by the Red Sox in the previous year's Fall Classic. The teams split the opening two games in St. Louis, as Chris Carpenter's strong Game 1 effort was matched by Oswalt edging out Mark Mulder in Game 2. The next three contests were tense, one-run affairs. Houston got victories in Games 3 and 4, and were poised to win the NLCS at home in Game 5 after building a two-run lead with one out to go in the ninth inning. Lidge struck out the first two batters he faced, but allowed a David Eckstein single and a walk to Jim Edmonds in front of that season's NL MVP, Albert Pujols. Pujols then crushed a mammoth homer to give the Cards the lead and, eventually, a win to force Game 6.

Nevertheless, the Astros would prevail in the sixth game, shaking off the shockwaves from Pujols' blast to advance to the World Series, where their magic ran out in a sweep at the hands of the Chicago White Sox.

Clockwise from far left: Oswalt helped the Astros punch their ticket to the 2005 World Series with a Game 6 NLCS clinch over St. Louis; once it opened in 2000, Minute Maid Park — which hosted the 2004 All-Star Game — and its retractable roof became an ideal place for fans to catch a game while escaping the Texas heat; Houston beat the Braves in the 2005 NLDS thanks to a walk-off, 18th-inning homer from Chris Burke.

KANSAS CITY ROYALS

Brett, the best player ever to wear "KC" on his cap, served as the inspirational leader on Royals clubs of the 1970s and '80s. It didn't hurt that he also won three batting titles.

SURROUNDED BY A CLASSIC STADIUM, stable ownership, and relatively little drama, the Kansas City Royals have long exuded the aura of a tradition-rich team, despite getting their start via expansion in 1969. From the start, club founder Ewing Kauffman sought to create a classy, consistent AL contender in the manner of the NL's Cardinals and Dodgers — and succeeded.

By 1979, a decade after the club's founding, Kansas City had already won three AL West titles thanks to a knack for plucking talented youngsters from teams that didn't realize what they had. Kansas City nabbed Amos Otis from the Mets, Hal McRae from the Reds, and also developed its own stars, like outfield speedster Willie Wilson. Most importantly, the Royals saw the talent hidden inside a second-round pick named George Howard Brett. With Brett serving as the franchise cornerstone — he won three batting titles, including a .390 mark in 1980 — the Royals became the Yankees' biggest rivals in the late '70s, facing New York in four memorable playoff series from 1976–80.

Kansas City lost the first three of those, but won the pennant in the fourth — only to fall in the World Series. In 1985, though, the Royals finally won it all, beating the Cardinals in the Fall Classic behind the gifted pitching of 21-year-old Cy Young winner Bret Saberhagen. The Royals faded quickly after their title, posting 18 losing seasons over the next 25 years, but lately Kansas City has returned to what worked in the 1970s: building from the ground up. And with draft picks like Eric Hosmer, the franchise boasts a bevy of talented youngsters.

Brett acknowledged the crowd after his fourth base hit on Aug. 17, 1980, raised his batting average to .401.

KC Royal Subjects

5 HITS allowed by Kansas City hurler Bret Saberhagen in Game 7 of the 1985 World Series. The Royals would go on to win the contest, 11-0, and top the St. Louis Cardinals for their first championship, coming back from an early two-game deficit.

2 RUNS down in their first-ever regular-season game on April 8, 1969, the Royals rallied to win the contest, 4-3, in 12 innings over the Minnesota Twins.

54 DOUBLES hit by Hal McRae in 1977, a club record. The part-time DH also put up a .298 average with 21 homers to help the Royals win the West for the second straight time. They would win a third division crown the following year.

2.16 ERA posted by 25-year-old right-hander Zack Greinke to lead the Major Leagues in his Cy Young Award–winning 2009 season. He also won 16 games.

52 STEALS recorded by Amos Otis during his second year in Kansas City in 1971. Overall, Otis would spend 14 seasons with the Royals, finishing high on the franchise career list in a number of categories, including runs (second) and hits (third).

1 CAUGHT STEALING recorded by Carlos Beltran in 2001 in 32 attempts. The Royals' center fielder led the league that season in stolen-base percentage.

KING GEORGE

All eyes were on George Brett in 1980. They watched as he walked to the batting cage to loosen up, sat rapt when he stepped into the box to smack another line drive, and crowded by his locker after games. The Kansas City Royals' third baseman was on fire, flirting with a .400 average during an MVP season — and no one wanted to miss a second.

Reporters followed Brett everywhere, seeking comment on his remarkable campaign. "I've never been this hot this long," he marveled in August. "I'm just going to try to keep telling myself that I'm hot. The thing I don't want to do is put pressure on myself. But it's hard not to think about what I'm hitting."

Baseball's other stars took notice, too. Before a game at Yankee Stadium in mid-July, New York slugger Reggie Jackson paused to watch a bit of Royals batting practice. "Just wanna watch Brett. I've never seen a man hitting .570," Jackson exaggerated. Brett went 7 for 14 during the three-game set, raising his actual average to .375.

Hampered by a handful of ailments, Brett started just 113 games in 1980, but when he did play, he was phenomenal. Chasing .400 all summer, he ended up at .390, the highest single-season average since Ted Williams hit .406 in 1941. Brett had hit well over .400 in June, July and August, striking out in just 22 of 449 at-bats. Said Yankees hitting coach Charlie Lau: "The only one who can get George out is George."

The only man ever to win a batting title in three different decades, George Brett was, as his skipper Whitey Herzog said, "one of the best clutch hitters in the history of the game." Utilizing a new-age swing with a one-handed release that hitting guru Lau had taught him, Brett captured his first crown with a .333 mark in 1976, narrowly edging out Kansas City teammate Hal McRae. That fall, the Royals played the Yankees in the ALCS for the first of three straight years, and although Kansas City would lose each series, Brett became a legend. His finest moment came in Game 3 of the '78 ALCS, when he hit three home runs, each of which tied the game or gave the Royals the lead — but Kansas City fell anyway, 6-5. Over three ALCS losses from 1976–78, Brett hit .375.

"He was clearly one of the best players of his generation, but he had a style that spanned the generations," sportscaster Bob Costas said. "There was nothing in the world that he would rather be doing than playing baseball every day."

Only 2009 American League MVP Joe Mauer has led the AL in the "slash stats" — batting average, on-base percentage and slugging percentage — since Brett managed the feat in 1980. Voted AL MVP in a landslide, Brett batted .343 in the playoffs that year to lead the Royals to the World Series, which they lost in six games. Five years later, Brett would finally grab that elusive ring, batting an impressive .370 in the 1985 Fall Classic as the Royals captured the franchise's first title.

THE K

Kauffman Stadium, affectionately referred to as "The K," has been around since 1973. Despite several renovations and upgrades to modernize the stadium, the design is considered to be among the most traditional in the sport. The ballpark boasts one of North America's largest scoreboards. In 2007, the Royals had a red seat placed among a sea of blue behind home plate to honor Negro Leagues legend Buck O'Neil, who played for and managed the Kansas City Monarchs. One fan, selected from a group of community nominees, is honored with the seat during each game. If it gets too hot out in the sun, the Pepsi Party Porch offers a terrace with a good view of the diamond.

Kauffman Stadium remains the only American League ballpark named for a person, rather than a sponsor, team or locale. Named for Ewing Kauffman, a pharmaceutical innovator and the club's original owner, The K features the world's largest publicly funded fountain beyond the right-field power alley and a 7,000-square foot Hall of Fame, opened in 2009, where the accomplishments of Royals greats George Brett, Bret Saberhagen and others are proudly displayed.

Honoring the club's original owner — Ewing Kauffman — Kauffman Stadium remains the only AL ballpark named after a person, rather than a place, team or sponsor.

The K combines modern amenities with deep tradition, and it also boasts the world's largest privately-funded fountain beyond the outfield fence.

SUCCESS CAME QUICKLY FOR SABERHAGEN. AT AGE 21, HE WHIFFED 158 BATTERS.

Saberhagen relocated his touch in 1987, and two years later, he went 23-6 with a strikeout-to-walk ratio of 4.49 and took home his second Cy Young Award. Saberhagen never walked 60 batters in a season, a consistent display of impeccable command, and although he had trouble staying healthy during his career, and at times had difficulty with the media, he remained well liked by fans and teammates alike.

REGAL REPEAT

It's uncanny how many similarities exist between the 1985 and '86 World Series. In both, the eventual champion lost the first two games at home, something that had never happened before. And in both, one play in the final inning of Game 6 turned the entire matchup on its head.

The Royals were down, 1-0, in the bottom of the ninth in Game 6, and it looked like a sure bet that the Cards were about to celebrate their title. Then, umpire Don Denkinger made a call that no St. Louis fan would ever forget: He ruled Kansas City's Jorge Orta safe at first on a play when replays showed he was clearly out. The Cards' response? Just like Boston in Game 6 of the '86 Series with pitcher Bob Stanley's wild pitch and Bill Buckner's error, the Cardinals collapsed, turning one blown call and one baserunner into a two-run rally. In Game 7, the Royals put the finishing touches on the Cards, crushing them, 11-0. Denkinger's name remains infamous to this day in St. Louis, but the Royals' surge — and the Cardinals' meltdown — was not exclusively a result of that call.

Series Most Valuable Player Bret Saberhagen pitched the decisive contest, his second complete game of the Series, but the Cy Young Award winner didn't need his best stuff that night. The Cardinals were so demoralized that they never stood a chance.

Saberhagen won Cy Young honors in '85 and also helped Kansas City win a world championship.

BOUNCING BACK

The encore to Bret Saberhagen's 20-6, 1985 Cy Young season was disappointing. In 1986, the 22-year-old Royals righty went 7-12. A sore arm was partly to blame, while others pointed to his naivety. "So much happens so quickly sometimes to young players," Royals second baseman Frank White said in 1987. "Sometimes they feel they are invincible. But they aren't."

Success had come quickly for Saberhagen in 1985. At age 21, he walked just 38 batters and whiffed 158 on his way to a world title. He was the ace of what baseball historian Bill James dubbed the best rotation of the 1980s.

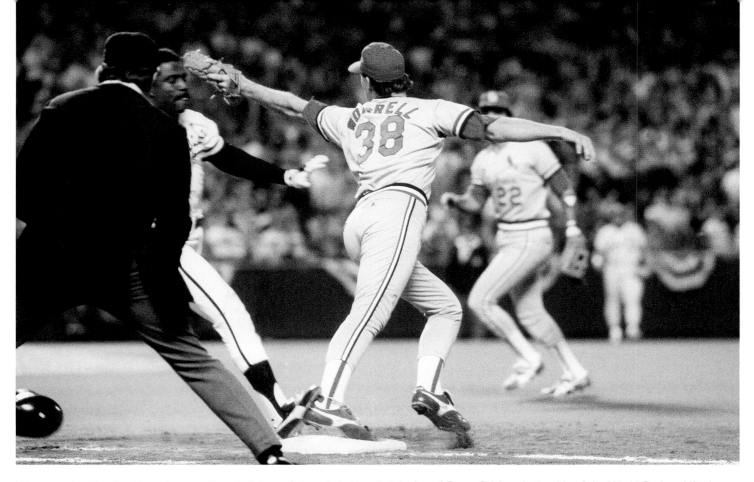

When umpire Don Denkinger incorrectly called Jorge Orta safe in the ninth inning of Game 6 (above), the tide of the World Series shifted dramatically and the Royals went on to win the Fall Classic. Brett (below, right) hoisted Series MVP Saberhagen off the ground after the right-hander tossed a complete game to seal Game 7 and finally bring the World Series crown to Kansas City.

LOS ANGELES ANGELS

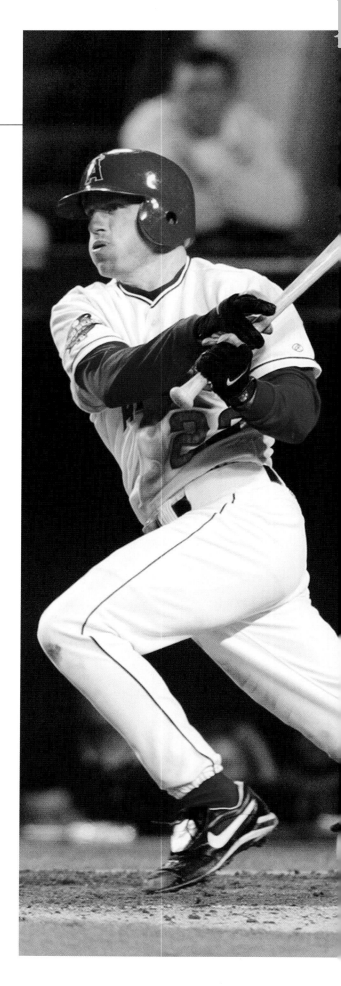

THE ANGELS, ALONG WITH THE Washington Senators (now the Texas Rangers), were Major League Baseball's first expansion team. They are also its most successful based on their regular season win-loss percentage, which is higher than that of any other expansion franchise. They were a contender right off the bat, too. As tenants at Dodger Stadium — which the Angels stubbornly insisted on calling "Chavez Ravine" — the Halos cruised to 86 wins and a third-place finish during their sophomore season of 1962. But playing in the Dodgers' shadow proved tough even after moving south to Orange County in 1966. In a constant attempt to redefine their fan base, the Angels are the only team ever to change their "city" name three times — from California to Anaheim to Los Angeles — without ever switching markets.

In 1971 the Angels cannily traded for a wild righty with massive untapped potential: Nolan Ryan. The Ryan Express became a runaway train in Anaheim, tossing four no-hitters in a three-year period and breaking MLB's single-season strikeout record with 383 in 1973. Powered by veterans like Bobby Grich, Don Baylor, Reggie Jackson, Rod Carew and Brian Downing, the Angels made brief playoff appearances in 1979, '82 and '86.

Manager Mike Scioscia led the club to its first-ever championship in 2002, and the good times continued the following year, when Arte Moreno purchased the team. Moreno's front office blended an outstanding farm system with judicious free-agent signings like Vladimir Guerrero, and the Angels finished first five times in a six-year span. With Albert Pujols now calling Anaheim home, Angels fans are hoping that another era of dominance is on the horizon.

The diminutive David Eckstein, standing 5 foot 6, epitomized the 2002 Angels' never-say-die attitude. He helped them defeat the Giants by hitting .310 in the World Series.

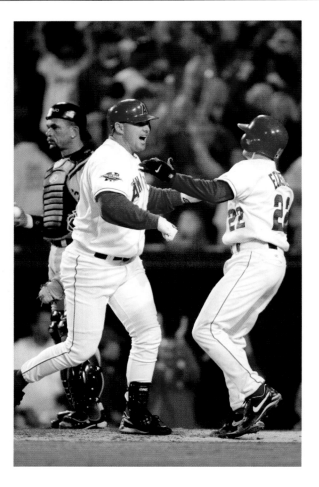

ONE FOR THE BOOKS

A longtime Halos star, Salmon (far left) took advantage of his opportunity in the World Series with a two-run, tie-breaking homer in Game 2, setting the trend for late-game heroics that would culminate with an Angels title.

Weeks afterward, Tim Salmon would still wake up sweating. His nightmare was preposterous but it felt real. The Angels weren't the world champions yet. They would have to keep playing.

It took a while for *everyone* to believe it, but the Angels really were the 2002 world champions.

The '02 Angels did not change baseball. But they absolutely transformed their franchise, and in a way that very few could have. The Halos led the Junior Circuit with a .282 batting average in '02, and even though they were 11th in the league in homers, they ranked fourth in runs. That offense helped the club win a Wild Card berth. And then the ALDS. And then the ALCS.

Then came the San Francisco Giants in the World Series. Down 3 games to 2, the Angels were on the brink of elimination when San Francisco took a 5-0 lead into the bottom of the seventh inning of Game 6.

Jack O'Connell, then of the *Hartford Courant*, had begun his game story by discussing the Giants' first world title since 1954. A fellow writer chimed in. "That's a good lead," O'Connell was told. "Don't fall in love with it."

Sure enough, the pesky Angels chipped away — a Scott Spiezio home run, another from Darin Erstad, a double from Troy Glaus — until the lead, and the game, was theirs. There would be a Game 7.

Manager Mike Scioscia chose rookie John Lackey to pitch on three days' rest in the decisive game. The Giants got on the board first with a run in the second, but a three-run double by Garret Anderson in the bottom of the third gave Lackey a 4-1 lead that he took into the sixth, when the bullpen took over. That was it. Four World Series wins, all of them in come-from-behind fashion. One of baseball's first expansion teams was now arguably its most successful.

"There aren't many days that go by when I don't think about that team," Salmon said years later. Many Angels fans surely agree.

HOT ROD

The Panama-born and New York–raised Rod Carew was already a surefire Hall of Famer when he arrived in Southern California via trade before the 1979 season. Carew had been selected to the All-Star Game in each of his first 12 Major League seasons (his streak would eventually reach 18, as he received the honor in all but his last season), won seven batting crowns, led the Junior Circuit in hits and intentional walks on three occasions, stole 40 bases twice, and won both Rookie of the Year and MVP awards.

Carew had come a long way from when he was discovered by a Twins scout while playing semi-pro sandlot ball in the Bronx, but he was determined to show Angels fans that he wasn't ready to hang up his spikes yet. In 1980, Carew used his loose grip and signature batting stance to rake at a .331 clip, while leading the Halos in hits, doubles, triples and steals at age 34. In his seven seasons as an Angel, Carew hit .314 with 180 extra-base hits and 82 steals in 834 games, a fitting conclusion to his Cooperstown-caliber career.

 Wing Men

.435 WINNING PERCENTAGE recorded by the Angels in their first season as a Major League club, in 1961. That mark still stands as a record high for an expansion team in its premiere campaign.

62 SAVES reached by Angels reliever Francisco Rodriguez in 2008 to break Bobby Thigpen's single-season record (57, set in 1990). K-Rod whiffed 77 batters in 68.1 innings pitched.

65 EXTRA-BASE HITS by Bobby Grich in 1979, his best season at the plate as an Angel. Grich finished that season at a .294 clip with 30 home runs and 30 doubles.

1.65 ERA posted by Dean Chance in 1964, when he won the American League Cy Young Award. Chance went 20-9 on the year and gave up just seven home runs in 278.1 innings pitched.

28 FIRST-PLACE VOTES for Tim Salmon in 1993 to take home the AL Rookie of the Year Award. With .283-31-95 totals, Salmon finished well ahead of Jason Bere and Aaron Sele.

2 HITS for Alex Johnson in three at-bats on the final day of the 1970 season to surpass Carl Yastrzemski for the AL batting title by a microscopic margin, .3289 to .3286.

After 12 stellar years with the Twins, the slap-hitting Carew landed in Anaheim in 1979 and proved that he wasn't over the hill. He made six more All-Star teams with the Angels.

A stern but well-liked skipper, Scioscia adds an even keel and stabilizing force to the Angels. He has won more games than any other manager in Halos history.

AN UNASSUMING LEADER

Mike Scioscia arrived in Anaheim at the turn of the millennium after the Angels had gone just 70-92 in 1999. A turnaround followed not much later.

The club went 82-80 with Scioscia at the helm in 2000, and finished under .500 just three times in his first 12 seasons. In 2002, the Angels won the World Series — the first championship in club history — with Scioscia leading the way. The win earned the former Big League backstop an AL Manager of the Year Award. He would take home another in 2009.

"It's his consistent approach to the day," said Rays Manager Joe Maddon, who served in the Angels organization for more than 30 years before becoming the Rays' skipper in 2006. "Whether they win or lose, the players see the same guy the next day. The players support that.

And, he is fearless. He is never afraid to answer questions, even when something goes wrong. It makes a difference to the players. They look at him as a guy who will put things on his shoulders."

Scioscia acknowledges none of those attributes, but admits that longevity and stability in the manager's office can be a big part of a successful franchise. He has been the Angels' manager for more than a decade and is signed through 2018. His winning percentage is well above .500, the highest ever by an Angels manager, and he has the most victories in club history — more than 1,000, which far surpasses the 625 posted by the club's first manager, Bill Rigney, in the 1960s. The players know Scioscia will be there in five years. They also know that if they don't play hard for him every day, they will be gone in five minutes. Relaxed, yet intense. That's how the Angels play because that's what Scioscia insists upon.

ANGELOLOGY

The franchise has only been around since 1961, but the Angels have had no shortage of colorful characters, home run heroes and kings of the hill. These are just some of the past stars to have donned the halo.

REGGIE JACKSON 1982–86
Jackson launched an American League–leading 39 home runs in his first season playing at the "Big A," while also earning his 12th All-Star selection and second Silver Slugger Award.

DON BAYLOR 1977–82
Baylor took home the AL MVP Award in 1979, as he led the Majors in runs scored and RBI, and ranked fourth in the Junior Circuit in longballs.

NOLAN RYAN 1972–79
After being traded from the Mets, the Major Leagues' all-time strikeout king accumulated 2,416 of his record 5,714 punchouts as a member of the Angels.

CHUCK FINLEY 1986–99
A five-time selection to the Midsummer Classic, Finley mixed his fastball with a devastating forkball to become one of the top left-handed power pitchers of the 1990s.

WALLY JOYNER 1986–91
The Angels' slugging first baseman managed to stand out from the crowd in a power-laden rookie class in 1986, hitting 22 homers and driving in 100 runs while playing solid defense.

DARIN ERSTAD 1996–2006
The first overall draft pick in 1995 out of the University of Nebraska hit 114 home runs as an Angel, including 25 in a 240-hit 2000 season.

BOBBY GRICH 1977–86
A standout high school quarterback, Grich led the AL in home runs (22) and slugging percentage (.543) in a strike-shortened 1981 season, all while continuing to provide top-flight second-base defense.

TIM SALMON 1992–2004, 2006
Named the Rookie of the Year in 1993, Salmon put up his best statistical season in 1995, finishing with a .330 average, 34 homers, 111 runs and 105 RBI.

VLADIMIR GUERRERO 2004–09
Guerrero, the franchise's biggest free-agent signing before Albert Pujols, won the Angels' second MVP Award in 2004, when he hit .337 with 39 homers.

BO BELINSKY 1962–64
In his fourth Major League start, Belinsky set down the visiting Baltimore Orioles without surrendering a hit. His nine-strikeout gem on May 5, 1962, was the first no-hitter thrown on the West Coast.

DEAN CHANCE 1961–66
The 23-year-old right-hander paced the AL in wins (20), innings pitched (278.1), complete games (15), shutouts (11) and ERA (1.65), while tallying the third-most strikeouts (207) in a Cy Young 1964 campaign.

TROY PERCIVAL 1995–2004
Percival's eight seasons with 30 or more saves gave him the clubhouse clout to take a leadership role, and the California native never hid from the responsibility.

MARK LANGSTON 1990–97
Able to field his position as well as anyone, and gifted with a famously quick pick-off move to first base, Langston won five of his seven Gold Glove Awards during his stint as an Angel.

FRANCISCO RODRIGUEZ 2002–08
Having never even reached 55 save opportunities in a single season, Rodriguez posted a record-setting 62-save campaign in 2008, striking out 77 in 68.1 innings.

Salmon (left) spent 14 seasons in Anaheim, starting with his Rookie of the Year campaign in 1993. Rodriguez saved an MLB single-season-record 62 games in 2008.

LOS ANGELES DODGERS

EVER SINCE THEIR DAYS IN Brooklyn, the Dodgers have been baseball's vanguard, the team that boldly leads the sport to frontiers where it has never been before. It was the Dodgers who integrated the national pastime by signing Jackie Robinson in 1945. It was the Dodgers who made baseball a sensation in Latin America with "Fernandomania." It was the Dodgers who signed MLB's first Japanese star, Hideo Nomo, and also introduced air travel, television and the high five to the sport. For good measure, they even employed the two most influential broadcasters of all time, Red Barber and Vin Scully. This innovative spirit has spawned tremendous box-office success, as the Dodgers have drawn more total fans than any sports franchise in history.

Named after the Brooklynites who dodged trolleys while crossing or playing in the streets, the Dodgers spent much of the early 1900s honing a reputation as clownish losers. But in 1941, they started winning and have hardly stopped since. The famed "Boys of Summer" slugged their way to six pennants in 10 years, including a world championship in 1955.

The winning continued after the move west to Los Angeles, with Sandy Koufax and company pitching the Dodgers to three championships between 1959 and '65. During the '70s and '80s, meanwhile, Los Angeles finished first or second 15 times in 20 years. The Dodgers then went into a franchise-long pennant drought lasting more than 20 years, but recently fans could rally behind superstars such as 2011 NL MVP runner-up Matt Kemp and 2011 Cy Young Award winner Clayton Kershaw.

No moment in Dodgers history has come close to approaching the day that Robinson took the field for the first time, breaking the Major League color barrier in 1947.

FERNANDOMANIA

The Mets added two extra ticket booths near the subway stop outside Shea Stadium in advance of Fernando Valenzuela's start in Queens on May 8, 1981. The season was young, but the Dodgers' rookie hurler was already the team's main attraction, and the Mets knew fans would flock to the ballpark for the game. Valenzuela, in his first six starts prior to the highly anticipated visit to the Big Apple, was 6-0 with five complete games and four shutouts.

In front of nearly 40,000 fans — up from just 5,653 spectators who had attended the previous day — Valenzuela almost let a first-inning lead slip away to the Mets over the next few innings. He put runners on base in each of the first three frames, but escaped unscathed. As was becoming customary, he walked off the hill a winner thanks to a complete-game shutout.

In SoCal, fans couldn't believe the 20-year-old was one of theirs. They gathered at Dodger Stadium in huge numbers to watch him twirl his epic screwball. The fervor even earned its own name: "Fernandomania."

In one of the greatest seasons by a rookie in Big League history, Dodgers games were taken over by spectacle and mania in 1981 thanks to Valenzuela. The left-hander helped push the club to the 1981 World Series title.

Although a labor dispute cut 50 days out of the middle of the 1981 season, Valenzuela had still impressed, including winning 13 of 25 starts and posting a 2.48 ERA. He was just as solid in the playoffs, helping the Dodgers advance to the World Series. There, he took the ball for a Game 3 start. After relinquishing a three-run lead in the third inning, he settled in to shut out the Yankees the rest of the way for a complete-game victory. In fact, after catcher Rick Cerone's two-out homer in that third frame, Valenzuela allowed just four hits, not letting the recaptured lead slip away again after the Dodgers took it for good in the fifth.

Fittingly, after his 1981 season performance, Valenzuela became the first pitcher to win both Rookie of the Year and Cy Young honors in the same season.

DYNAMIC DUO

Ballplayers, fans, managers and just about everyone who had ever watched ball meet bat were in agreement that Sandy Koufax was pitching better than anyone had before him. The Dodgers' southpaw won the pitching Triple Crown in the National League in 1963, 1965 and 1966 and was the unanimous Cy Young Award winner all three years. He twirled three no-hitters and a perfect game during that span, won an MVP Award, set the modern single-season strikeout record, recorded the most K's in a World Series game, was named MVP of the 1963 Fall Classic and made believers on both coasts.

While he was at the peak of his powers, it seemed a shock whenever anyone even scratched a hit off of Koufax, let alone handed him a loss. Given the price he paid for every pitch with his arthritic arm, Koufax made each one count. In addition to posting the lowest ERA of his brilliant career in 1966, he guided his club to its third NL pennant in four years, going 7-0 with a 1.69 ERA against the Dodgers' two main rivals, the Giants and Pirates. The arthritis eventually forced his retirement after that '66 season, but Koufax was still elected to the Hall of Fame five years later in his first year of eligibility.

Alongside Koufax, Don Drysdale was part of a historic pitching duo at the top of the Dodgers' rotation for years. From 1956–66, Drysdale and Koufax teamed up to form a one-two punch that simply could not be bested. Like his left-handed counterpart, Drysdale seemed to get better with age. He posted an ERA under 3.00 in seven of nine seasons from 1960–68 with steadily shrinking walk rates, and won the Cy Young Award in 1962, when he put

Drysdale (left) and Koufax gave the Dodgers arguably the best one-two punch the game has ever seen when they dominated NL foes — and, often in the World Series, AL teams — during the 1960s. Fittingly, both were elected to the Hall of Fame.

Few Major League ballparks can compare with the view fans get at Dodger Stadium. The ballpark, now one of the oldest in the league, has plenty to offer the patrons who pack its seats on a regular basis.

up 25 wins and a 2.83 earned run average. Although he would pitch for a few more years than Koufax — and have a longer wait on the ballot — Drysdale joined Koufax in Cooperstown in 1984.

BELIEVE IT

The Los Angeles Dodgers entered the 1988 World Series as underdogs against the powerhouse Oakland Athletics, and became even more of a long shot when injuries left soon-to-be-named NL MVP Kirk Gibson — who had hurt both his right knee and left hamstring during the NLCS — unable to play. It was no surprise, then, when Oakland took early control of Game 1, and handed a 4-3 lead to Hall of Fame closer Dennis Eckersley. The first two Dodgers made outs in the ninth before pinch-hitter Mike Davis, a .196 batter, worked an unlikely walk — just the 11th free pass Eck gave up that season. That brought up the pitcher's spot. Utility infielder Dave Anderson

L.A.'s Finest

A hobbled Gibson gave baseball fans a memory for the ages when he limped around the bases after taking Eckersley deep in Game 1 of the 1988 Series.

20 INNINGS thrown by spitballing right-hander Burleigh Grimes on April 30, 1919. Despite his effort, the team managed just a 9-9 tie against the Philadelphia Phillies.

78,672 FANS attended the Dodgers' Opening Day game in Los Angeles in 1958 at the Los Angeles Memorial Coliseum, their first regular-season home game following the club's move to the West Coast.

84 SAVE OPPORTUNITIES in a row converted by Eric Gagne, a Major League record. His final save of the streak came on July 3, 2004, against the rival Angels.

9 PITCHES needed by Sandy Koufax against the New York Mets in the first inning on June 30, 1962, to strike out the side. Eight innings later, Koufax completed the first of his four career no-hitters, finishing with 13 K's.

9 SEASONS from 1973–81 that the Dodgers' infield was shared by first baseman Steve Garvey, second baseman Davey Lopes, shortstop Bill Russell and third baseman Ron Cey. Los Angeles won four NL pennants and a World Series title in that time.

3 GOLD GLOVE AWARDS won by first baseman Gil Hodges from 1957–59. The eight-time All-Star could hit, too, collecting 370 career home runs.

was sent to the on-deck circle as a decoy, but Dodgers Manager Tommy Lasorda had an ace up his sleeve.

Gibson had been taking practice swings off a tee in the clubhouse and, to everyone's surprise, he limped to the plate with the game on the line. Gibson fought off pitch after pitch, but a weak hobble toward first base after a couple of foul grounders brought into question whether he could reach safely even on a ball hit to the outfield. As it turned out, he didn't need to.

Eckersley tried to sneak in a 3-2 backdoor slider for strike three, but Gibby was ready, and with a one-handed swing, pulled Eck's offering into the right-field pavilion for a walk-off homer. It was not only arguably the most dramatic and unlikely hit in World Series history, but also the first come-from-behind, walk-off homer ever in the Fall Classic. To this day, Gibson remains the only man to hit a game-winning World Series home run in a situation in which his team would have lost if he had made an out. The win lit a fire under the Dodgers, who went on to take the Series in five games.

THE DUKE OF FLATBUSH

During the 1950s, whenever New Yorkers argued about whether the best center fielder in the city was Willie Mays or Mickey Mantle, Brooklynites were quick to step in with their own answer: Edwin "Duke" Snider. While he may not receive as much attention as his counterparts, the blue-eyed, silver-haired Dodgers slugger was arguably the best of the three fabulously gifted players when they all roamed center field in New York in the middle of the 20th century.

Even at his best, Snider often found himself overshadowed in the five seasons that he shared New York with Mays and Mantle — 1951 and 1954–57. In '54, he slugged 40 home runs, scored 120 runs, drove in 130 and batted a career-best .341, but lost both the batting title and the NL pennant to Mays and the Giants during the last few weeks of the season.

Yet, while Snider had neither Mays' exuberance nor Mantle's mystique, his 194 home runs over those five seasons topped Mays' 183 and Mantle's 163. Snider also led the trio with 560 RBI. And for the 1950s as a whole, it was the Duke who led all Major League players in home runs and RBI.

As graceful and gifted as he could be, Snider's game was not without flaws. For one, he was a profoundly streaky hitter, and was thus prone to slumps. This caused the moody Snider to sometimes lash out, affecting his play on the field. "He could get very upset," Dodgers teammate Pee Wee Reese once said. "He would go 0 for 4 and he'd be standing in the outfield, but he wouldn't be thinking about the hitter. He'd be thinking about not getting a base hit."

As a result of the Dodgers' move west in 1957, the left-handed slugger would have to take aim at the Los Angeles Coliseum's 440-foot death valley in right-center. That, combined with knee surgery, effectively ended Snider's career as a superstar at age 31. When he left the game in 1964, his 407 homers ranked 10th all time. It was an impressive career, but fans could only wonder what might have been.

With Mantle and Mays as his competition in New York, Snider still held his own.

117

MIAMI MARLINS

ONLY THE SECOND FRANCHISE ever to win two World Series titles in its first 11 years of existence — the A's are the other — the Marlins have had three distinct rebirths during their young history. Founded by video-rental mogul Wayne Huizenga as an expansion club in 1993, the early years of the Marlins saw unexpected contributions from the likes of aging knuckleballer Charlie Hough, who won the first game in franchise history, and Jeff Conine, who made the All-Star squad in 1994 and '95 and became known as "Mr. Marlin" during his eight years with the club.

By 1997, the first great Marlins team was ready for prime time. Catcher Charles Johnson, pitcher Livan Hernandez and shortstop Edgar Renteria formed the young homegrown core, and they were bolstered by the addition of veterans Moises Alou, Al Leiter, Kevin Brown and Gary Sheffield. The Marlins captured a championship in just their fifth season, but the vets' salaries proved too unwieldy and the roster was broken up following the title. Within six years, though, the rebuilding process was complete, and the Marlins won the 2003 World Series behind a different crop of homegrown stars that included Josh Beckett and Miguel Cabrera.

Cabrera and Beckett were eventually traded to the Tigers and Red Sox, respectively, but the Marlins spent the early 2010s assembling what they hope will become their third distinct championship roster, this one led by Hanley Ramirez and Josh Johnson. In 2012, the franchise embarked on a bold new reinvention. It changed its name to the Miami Marlins, adopted new team colors, moved into a brand new retractable roof stadium, signed coveted free agents Jose Reyes, Heath Bell and Mark Buehrle, and even traded for Manager Ozzie Guillen, who seems certain to keep things interesting in South Florida for years to come.

The Marlins stood on the lines for two Fall Classics — each of which the Fish won — in their first 11 seasons as a ballclub.

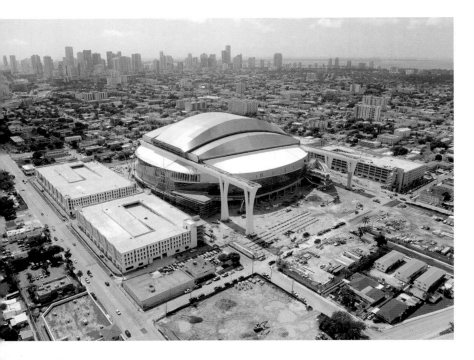

A HOME OF THEIR OWN

The Marlins' dynamic new ballpark was a work in progress before the 2012 season, and team mascot Billy the Marlin was there — hard hat and all — to supervise.

Major League Baseball has been going through a ballpark youth movement since the early 1990s. Thirteen new stadiums have opened since 2000, and when the Marlins joined the renaissance in the spring of 2012, 20 of the 30 Big League venues were less than 20 years old. Even classics like Kansas City's Kauffman Stadium, host of the 2012 All-Star Game, have benefitted from digital-age upgrades. And the granddaddy of them all, Fenway Park, incorporated new touches in celebration of its 100th birthday in 2012.

But what does it take to build a new ballpark, or make an old one feel new? Money, creativity and patience — not to mention plenty of luck. The path is different in every city, of course. But when real estate, politics and hundreds of millions of dollars are involved, the process is sure to be full of unanticipated wrinkles and multiple hurdles. While negotiations were taking place with the city of Miami, the Marlins watched excellent new ballparks rise across the country — in 2004, Citizens Bank Park in Philadelphia and Petco Park in San Diego, a new Busch Stadium in St. Louis in 2006, Nationals Park in 2008, two New York debuts in 2009 and Target Field in Minneapolis the following year.

Learning from what they saw, Marlins brass knew they needed a home of their own for the club, rather than sharing a stadium with the NFL's Miami Dolphins. Establishing a residence is a pivotal step in creating a team's identity, and that's just what the Marlins sought to do. What better way, then, to reinvent and reinvigorate a brand than to make its venue unique, flavorful and attractive as a destination? Sure, a name change and uniform tweak can provide some sense of transformation, but nothing makes a splash like a new ballpark, especially one designed with such a charismatic locale in mind.

Miami is a playful city, bursting with sound and sea and color, hence the bold touches all over the Marlins' new park. There's a 60-foot sculpture, designed by artist Red Grooms, behind the left-center field wall that whirls and shines when the home team homers. Behind each on-deck circle lies a 450-gallon-plus aquarium. During the offseason before the park's inaugural season, team President David Samson was fixated on a smaller detail that should make Marlins fans happy: He sat in each of the new park's 37,000 seats to make sure the view was perfect.

EARLY RISERS

Some team was bound to take an unorthodox route to the championship sooner or later. Enter the 1997 Florida Marlins, the first Wild Card team to win a World Series. The Marlins' seven-game tussle with the Indians, though it featured two smaller-market teams, was one of the most remarkable Fall Classics ever — and it was topped off by a sensational finale. "Had that been the Yankees and Mets playing, it would have gone down as one of the greatest World Series in history," Jim Leyland, the Marlins' skipper in 1997, told MLB.com 10 years later.

Counsell (above), who just two innings earlier had hit the sacrifice fly that tied Game 7 and prolonged the 1997 World Series, crossed the plate with the winning run in the 11th after Renteria (right) lined a single to center to give the Marlins their first championship.

Historians may recall the '97 Series as a sloppy one, with the middle three games at Cleveland's Jacobs Field played in poor weather conditions. But the contests rarely lacked entertainment and, of course, there was the drama of a Game 7. In the ninth inning of the decisive game, the Indians were just two outs away from their first title since 1948, but reliever Jose Mesa couldn't close it out. Instead, he allowed Moises Alou to lead off the frame with a single. Mesa retired Bobby Bonilla on a swinging strikeout, and the Indians were a double play from a World Series title. But catcher Charles Johnson defied that outcome with a single that advanced Alou to third, and with one out, Craig Counsell plated Alou on a sacrifice fly to right field, prolonging the game, the Series and the Marlins' title hopes.

Second-year shortstop Edgar Renteria came up with two outs and the bases full in the 11th. He buckled his knee on the first slider thrown to him by Cleveland's Charles Nagy, later saying that it was a ploy to induce Nagy to throw the pitch again. Nagy did throw another one, and Renteria lined it up the middle for a walk-off win. The Marlins were champs in just their fifth season. "I still think about it," Renteria said in 2007. "It's something that you dream about."

The 2003 Marlins celebrate a walk-off win (top). Ramirez (above) produced a 30-homer, 30-steal campaign in 2008.

Go Fish

42,344 **FANS** attended the Marlins' first home game on April 5, 1993. The Marlins topped the Los Angeles Dodgers, 6-3.

2 **WALKS** allowed by southpaw Al Leiter in his no-hitter against the Rockies on May 11, 1996. The no-no was a first for the franchise — and Leiter.

9 **BASES ON BALL** recorded by right-hander A.J. Burnett in his no-hitter against the San Diego Padres on May 12, 2001. Burnett also struck out seven batters, completing the feat in 129 pitches.

35 **CONSECUTIVE GAMES** with a hit by Luis Castillo during the 2002 season. Castillo, who batted .305 on the year, set a record for second basemen with the string.

28 **PICKS** into the first round of the 1992 draft when the Marlins made Charles Johnson their first-ever selection. Johnson would go on to become a two-time All-Star catcher.

3 **SEASONS** into his career when phenom shortstop Hanley Ramirez joined the 30/30 club with 33 home runs and 35 steals on the 2008 season.

OVERCOMING THE ODDS

They didn't knock the ball around — or out of — the park like the Red Sox had. They didn't even out-hit the Yanks. And they didn't have the hearts of all Americans beating in tune with their own, a fete the Cubs enjoyed.

No, the Marlins didn't win the 2003 World Series by being flashy, dominant or even particularly lovable. They won by being timely. Timely hits, timely pitching, timely fielding; everything in the universe conspired just right for the Marlins — a clear Series underdog — to emerge victorious on the hallowed grounds of Yankee Stadium.

The 2003 Fall Classic will not be remembered for any Carlton Fisk or Bill Mazeroski moments. Instead, the Marlins' place in baseball lore will mention a team that scored more than half of its runs in the Series with two outs. They'll be remembered for somehow being able to overcome the Yankees staff's 2.13 Series ERA, the best for a Fall Classic loser since the St. Louis Browns in 1944. From Juan Pierre's heroics in Game 1 to the bullpen's highwire act and Miguel Cabrera's homer off Roger Clemens in Game 4 to Brad Penny's clutch work with the bat — in addition to his arm — there are plenty of surreal moments for Fish fans to fondly recall. And, of course, no one will stop talking about a 23-year-old named Josh Beckett being sent out for the biggest game of his life on just three days' rest, and proceeding to fire a shutout in the Bronx in Game 6.

The 2003 Marlins will be remembered for a long time. After all, how do you forget the unforgettable?

The Fish completed their underdog story in 2003 with a World Series title, the franchise's second since its debut in 1993.

MILWAUKEE BREWERS

WISCONSINITES WERE heartbroken when the Braves left for Atlanta in 1966, but local auto dealer Allan "Bud" Selig made sure that void didn't last long. By 1970, Milwaukee was a Big League city again thanks to the future commissioner, who purchased the expansion Seattle Pilots and moved them to his hometown. Rebranded as the Brewers, the team didn't win more than 74 games in any of its first four seasons in Milwaukee. But the club reached a turning point on Opening Day 1974 when 18-year-old Robin Yount made his debut just months after being drafted with the third overall pick.

The no-nonsense Yount would become the leader of a crew of burly sluggers who seemed right at home in the city where Harley-Davidson was founded. In 1982, everything fell into place for "Harvey's Wall-bangers," named after skipper Harvey Kuenn. Sweet-swinging lefty Cecil Cooper, sparkplug Paul Molitor, slugger Gorman Thomas and soft-spoken outfielder Ben Oglivie littered the American League leaderboards and formed a potent offense. Mostly, though, the pennant-winning Brewers were propelled by Yount, who led the league in hits, doubles, OPS and total bases, while also winning a Gold Glove at shortstop. The Brewers lost that '82 Series, though, and it would be another 26 years before they played postseason ball again. In mid-2008 Milwaukee traded for one of MLB's best pitchers, CC Sabathia, who carried them to a dramatic Wild Card berth by going 11-2 with a 1.65 ERA over the season's final three months. Although Sabathia would depart after the season, the team's core of young stars — Ryan Braun, Yovani Gallardo and Rickie Weeks — brought home an NL Central title in 2011.

The 2011 Brew Crew made it all the way to the NLCS against the Cardinals — Milwaukee's first trip to a League Championship Series since 1982. The Brewers' run ended there in six games, but not before energizing the fan base.

Yount is still considered one of the most beloved players of all time in Milwaukee. He spent his entire 20-year career with the Brew Crew and, in 1999, became the first player to enter the Hall of Fame as a Brewer.

BLUE-COLLAR HERO

Although Milwaukee may not have Philadelphia's Liberty Bell or the picture-perfect weather of Los Angeles, it does have its own legacy and circle of personalities that have helped shape its character.

Take away Philly's history or L.A.'s sunshine, and it just wouldn't be the same. Milwaukeeans feel the same way about the legacy of their beloved adopted son, Robin Yount. To put it in simpler terms, Yount and the city go together like another famous Milwaukee duo: beers and brats.

"I think people in Wisconsin want you to be one of them. Milwaukeeans want you to convince them that you like being here," said Hall of Famer Don Sutton, who played for the Brewers for more than two years. "You have to convince them that you're playing hard and you're trying to do your best."

Yount did just that, every day, for 20 seasons and 20 consecutive Spring Trainings. He had always been "The Kid." A young man freshly plucked from his high school prom, he quickly found himself fielding scalding grounders rocketing off Major League bats.

Yount provided Milwaukee with a sense of pride not felt since the heyday before the Braves moved to Atlanta. In 1974, at age 18, he became the Brewers' starting shortstop and one of the youngest everyday players in Big League history. A career .285 hitter, he was a three-time All-Star and became the first player to enter the Hall of Fame as a Brewer in 1999.

"He was a working class kind of player," said Cecil Cooper, who played with Yount in the '80s. "He was a throwback to the old days."

Prognosticator Henry Aaron called Yount the best prospect in baseball back in 1975, and Hammerin' Hank knew what he was talking about. Yount earned the MVP Award twice — in 1982 and '89 — at two different positions (he moved to the outfield in 1985). He could have played in any city he desired, but he preferred to stay put.

HARVEY'S WALLBANGERS

Nicknamed "Harvey's Wallbangers" for their slugging prowess at the plate and no-holds-barred play in the field, the 1982 Brewers, under the direction of Manager Harvey Kuenn, led the Major Leagues in home runs while also pacing the American League in runs batted in and runs scored.

Center fielder Gorman Thomas, the epitome of the rough-and-tumble Wallbangers, paved the way with a league-high 39 home runs and 112 RBI, playing most of the season with an assortment of injuries sustained during his running, diving and wall-banging pursuit of

every ball hit his way. Cecil Cooper hit 32 homers and drove in 121 runs; Ben Oglivie hit 34 home runs and drove in 102. Yount, who went on to win the first of his two AL Most Valuable Player Awards in his 20-year Hall of Fame career, hit 29 home runs, 12 triples and a league-leading 46 doubles.

The Brewers came into the 1982 season favored to win the AL East, but they struggled out of the gate. With the team in the midst of an 8-14 slump, General Manager Harry Dalton fired Manager Buck Rodgers and replaced him with Kuenn, a Wisconsin native and the team's long-time hitting coach.

Kuenn simply let his Wallbangers go out and play. Baseball was not a matter of life and death for him, and his players responded to their manager's laid-back, almost fatherly approach. Harvey's Wallbangers hit 35 home runs during a 15-game stretch in June, a Major League record at the time, and won 20 of 27 games that month while closing in on first place.

The Brewers would eventually grab the division lead and hold off the Orioles by just one game to earn a postseason berth. After losing the first two games of the ALCS against the Angels, the Brew Crew returned home to pull off the unthinkable — win three straight contests to become the first team to win a League Championship Series after trailing 2 games to none.

The Brewers would then take the National League champion St. Louis Cardinals to seven games before losing, 6-3, in the deciding game of the 1982 World Series, which was dubbed "The Suds Series" because of each city's solid reputation for brewing.

"That's what you play for all your life," Yount said. "That's why you take all those ground balls and all that batting practice for years and years. Just to be able to get to that point. We were so fortunate that we got to experience that."

Kuenn began the 1982 season as the club's hitting coach, but got the chance to manage when the team fired Buck Rodgers. The hard-hitting "Harvey's Wallbangers" were born, and the club went on to reach the '82 Fall Classic.

127

Molitor spent the first 15 seasons of his career with Milwaukee, leading the league in runs scored three times and racking up five All-Star selections during that span.

 **Milwaukee's Best**

39 **CONSECUTIVE GAMES** with a hit by Paul Molitor in 1987. His streak was the longest in the Junior Circuit since Joe DiMaggio hit in 56 straight in 1941.

5 **PICKS** into the first round of the 2005 draft that the Brewers snatched up University of Miami slugger Ryan Braun. During his 2007 NL Rookie of the Year campaign, Braun blasted 34 homers in 451 at-bats.

707 **RUNS** scored by the Brew Crew in 1998, their first year in the NL. As part of a realignment, Milwaukee moved to the Senior Circuit from the AL.

45 **HOME RUNS** recorded by Richie Sexson during the 2003 season. Coupled with his 45 blasts in 2001, Sexson became the first Brewer to collect two 40-homer campaigns.

755 **HOMERS** stroked by Hank Aaron during his career, a mark that stood for more than 30 years until it was broken by Barry Bonds. Aaron hit his final homer on July 20, 1976, as a Brewer.

18 **STRIKEOUTS** recorded by Ben Sheets for the Brewers on May 16, 2004. Sheets finished second in the National League that season with 264 total strikeouts.

ON THE BRINK

The Brewers started setting a foundation for an eventual 2011 division crown soon after the 2010 season ended. The acquisition of right-handed pitchers Shaun Marcum and Zack Greinke to join forces with staff ace Yovani Gallardo, as well as veteran relievers Takashi Saito and LaTroy Hawkins, made it evident that General Manager Doug Melvin was serious about addressing the team's major weakness — pitching.

The optimism took a bit of a hit when the Brewers were swept at Cincinnati to open the season. Closer John Axford blew a save — and the game — in the opener.

The Brewers struggled to get over the .500 mark in April, settling for a 13-12 record after the first month. But Greinke and outfielder Corey Hart came back from injuries in early May, and the Brewers started heating up, going 21-7 from May 7 through June 6, the best record in baseball for those 28 games.

Milwaukee made its big move during a nine-game homestand after the All-Star break, starting with a 3-2 win over the Cubs on July 26. All of the Brewers' runs were scored in the first inning. They went on to sweep the Cubs and did the same against the Astros.

Milwaukee's dominance at home continued late in the year, when the Brewers took six of seven games from the Pirates and Dodgers. As the Brewers kept rolling, they built a 10.5-game first-place lead, the largest in team history. The Crew finished August with a 21-7 mark again — matching the same record earlier in the year — one win short of the club record for victories in that month. They would clinch the division with a 4-1 win over the Marlins on Sept. 23.

High drama played out in the NLDS, as the Brewers and Diamondbacks needed all five games before Nyjer Morgan's extra-inning, walk-off single sent the Brewers to an NLCS date with St. Louis. There, shaky pitching and defense cost Milwaukee; the Brewers fell in six games, the second time a World Series berth escaped the club's grasp.

Fans have flocked to the Brewers' Miller Park in droves since the stadium opened in 2001, and players like Gallardo — who served as the ace of the staff during the 2011 playoff run — have given them reason to keep coming back.

MINNESOTA TWINS

FIRST IN WASHINGTON AND LATER in Minnesota, the Twins have always found themselves trying to compete with baseball's bigger-market teams — yet often doing surprisingly well at it. The Washington Senators hired Manager Clark Griffith in 1912, and the following year, riding a 36-7 performance by the legendary Walter Johnson, they barely missed a pennant. A decade later, Johnson helped the Senators capture two flags, and each year they played in an extraordinarily tight World Series — winning in seven games in 1924 and losing in seven in '25. In 1961, the team moved to Minnesota, where slugger Harmon Killebrew, signed as a 17-year-old prodigy in 1954, finally came into his own. Killebrew won five home run titles from 1962–69, and aided by a pair of hitting machines — Tony Oliva and Rod Carew — the Twins posted 12 winning seasons during their first 17 in Minnesota.

In 1986, when Tom Kelly took over as manager and Oliva as hitting coach, singles-hitting outfielder Kirby Puckett became a power threat overnight. With his ear-to-ear smile, gregarious personality and all-out play, Puckett became the most popular player in franchise history, leading the underdog club to memorable titles in 1987 and '91. In 2002 Kelly passed the baton smoothly to his third base coach Ron Gardenhire, who has continued Minnesota's winning ways. Despite operating on a middle-of-the-pack payroll, the Twins — with the likes of two-time Cy Young winner Johan Santana, 2006 MVP Justin Morneau and 2009 MVP Joe Mauer — won six AL Central crowns in Gardenhire's first decade as skipper.

RIGHT ON TARGET

The open-air Target Field is full of features that have helped it earn a reputation as one of the best parks in the game, from fine architecture to a beautiful downtown vista to a massive "Minnie and Paul" logo that lights up.

Wherever they come from, die-hard Twins fans who endured 28 seasons cocooned inside the ground-bound zeppelin known as the Metrodome — more suitable for a football team such as the NFL's Minnesota Vikings, who just so happened to share the venue with the Twins — are surely enjoying their still-mint Target Field, which opened in 2010. Come rain, shine or snow, fans have packed the stadium game after game. In its first two full seasons of existence, Target Field welcomed nearly 6.5 million fans through its turnstiles — comfortably above 3 million each season — and the Twins placed third and second in the American League in attendance those years, respectively.

What makes that nugget even more impressive is that the Twins faithful kept showing up in droves despite a disappointing 2011 season. Finishing with just 63 wins, the Twins were out of playoff contention for the majority of the year.

Among cold-weather Big League cities with roofless stadiums (Cleveland, Detroit, Chicago, Boston, Denver, New York and Pittsburgh), Minneapolis isn't too far from the pack; the average daily temperature in April — 46 degrees — is just two degrees cooler than in Denver and Detroit, and just three degrees below Boston, Chicago and Cleveland, a good indicator that concerns over having an open-air stadium in Minnesota were overblown.

Still, the Twins are committed to providing a comfortable fan experience during less-than-ideal weather. Spectators are able to retreat to heated concessions, restrooms, restaurants and lounges on each level of the park. Target Field's canopy provides added protection for thousands of fans.

And of course, anytime the Twins are still alive come October, nobody's going to be complaining about weather.

THE BIG TRAIN

Before Randy Johnson, Roger Clemens, Nolan Ryan or Bob Feller forged careers as the premier power pitchers of their eras, there was Walter Johnson, whose name epitomized what a fireballer was for future generations.

Over a brilliant 21-year Major League career, all spent with Washington, Johnson would post numbers unfathomable to today's fans — 417 wins, 666 games started, 531 complete games, 110 shutouts (all American League records), 3,509 strikeouts and a 2.17 earned run average. He also led the league in strikeouts 12 times, won at least 20 games for 10 straight seasons, tossed three shutouts in four days in 1908 and posted 16 consecutive wins during one stretch in 1912.

Despite this success, there is no telling how many games the hard-throwing righty might have won had he pitched for even an average team, as Washington often found itself firmly entrenched in the AL's second division. Of his 531 complete games, 114 went for losses.

Standing 6 foot 1 and weighing close to 200 pounds, Johnson was an imposing sight for most of the batsmen of his day. But it was his pitching motion that was most distinct. He was called a sidearmer, but his delivery was more underhanded as he let the pitch go from a position very nearly off his knee.

"It took years to make a pitcher out of me," Johnson would say. "Before that I was a thrower."

Johnson finally got a chance to participate in a World Series in 1924, after 17 years in the Majors. He actually lost the first and fifth games of the Series, but pitched four innings of relief in Game 7 and was credited with the victory that gave Washington its only championship.

On the day after Johnson announced his retirement as an active player, *The Washington Post* editorialized: "In the latter sense Walter Johnson was an inspiration to his colleagues in the game and to thousands of boys whose baseball days were limited to the sandlots. What Walter Johnson did was always worth emulating either as a player or a man."

Johnson's career marks are colored by the fact that for years he played on teams that were middling at best, but his Game 7 win in the 1924 World Series gave the Senators the title.

Twins Hall of Famers

ROD CAREW . . . . Racked up 3,053 career hits and was selected to 18 consecutive All-Star Games.

GOOSE GOSLIN . . . . . . Hit .316 as a powerful slugger who earned a reputation for coming through in the clutch.

BUCKY HARRIS . . . . . . The future skipper hit .300 in his first full year.

WALTER JOHNSON . . . . Rode a sweeping fastball to 3,508 strikeouts and 417 career wins.

HARMON KILLEBREW . . The popular hitter reached 40 homers eight times and collected 573 total.

KIRBY PUCKETT . . . . . With an infectious smile, he led Minnesota on and off the field, winning two world championships.

SAM RICE . . . . Compiled a .322 batting average and 2,987 hits.

Manager Ron Gardenhire (center, right) and the Twins opened Target Field on April 12, 2010, by beating the visiting Boston Red Sox, 5-2.

135

KILLER INSINCT

Killebrew could mash with the best of them, and when he retired, his 573 career home runs ranked fifth in Major League history. In June 1967, he hit a longball that traveled a reported 520 feet, setting a Twins record.

In 1954, the Washington Senators signed 17-year-old Harmon Killebrew for $30,000, a bonus so large that the rules of the day prohibited the team from sending him to the Minors. He then spent five excruciating years on the bench before he was deemed ready to play in 1959 — and promptly led the American League with 42 home runs. He went on to win five more home run titles and knocked in 100 runs nine times. Needless to say, Killebrew never rode the pine again. Despite playing in the heart of a pitching-dominated era, "Killer" ended his career with 573 round-trippers — fifth on the all-time list when he retired in 1975. Consistent power was the name of Killebrew's game. Although he finished with such a gaudy total, never once did Killebrew top 50 homers in a single season. The only players to finish with more career home runs without a 50-homer campaign, as of 2012, are long-time Reds and Orioles slugger Frank Robinson and the great Hank Aaron.

Long known as one of baseball's most amiable players, Killebrew always made a point of helping others, even after he fell on financial hard times himself. In 1977, Killebrew established the Danny Thompson Memorial Golf Tournament to raise money for research to find a cure for leukemia — the disease that killed his teammate, Thompson, at age 29. It was just the first on a long list of charity ventures that Killebrew, who passed away in 2011, worked on after his career ended.

TWIN CITY TWO-STEP

Imagine a decibel level so overwhelming that your ears hurt. Imagine a wall of noise so thick that it clings to you like a second skin. Such was the sensory overload inside the Metrodome during Game 7 of the 1991 World Series, where the Twins and Braves waged a battle so fierce that many regard it as the greatest Fall Classic ever.

One of the most remarkable features of that Series was that neither team lost at home. The Twins had home-field advantage, which meant the Series was in a dead heat going into the final game.

And talk about showdowns: Minnesota's 36-year-old veteran Jack Morris took on Atlanta's 24-year-old wunderkind John Smoltz. *The ace of the past meets the ace of the future.* Morris embraced the drama. "In the words of the late, great Marvin Gaye," he said on the eve of Game 7, "let's get it on."

Had Game 7 of the 1991 World Series turned out to be anything but a classic, it would have been a bitter disappointment. Four of the first six games were decided by one run, three of them in walk-off fashion, two in extra innings. Were it not for Kirby Puckett, who hit a walk-off homer in the 11th inning of Game 6, Morris and the Twins might never even have had the chance to play in a Game 7. Puckett's heroics kept the Twins going for one more game. And he made it possible for the gripping one-on-one battle between Morris and Smoltz that baseball fans still talk about to this day.

For nine innings, neither team crossed the plate. The Braves blew a chance to take the lead in the eighth when Lonnie Smith failed to score from first base on Terry Pendleton's double.

Soon afterward, Smoltz was removed from the game, the consternation obvious on his face as skipper Bobby Cox ambled out to the mound. Morris, meanwhile, continued to post zeroes on the scoreboard, including in the top of the 10th, when he retired Atlanta on a mere eight pitches. That helped set the stage for the Twins' dramatic rally in the bottom of the 10th. Dan Gladden started it with a double. After Knoblauch moved Gladden to third with a sacrifice, the Braves intentionally walked Puckett and Kent Hrbek to load the bases. Up next was pinch-hitter Gene Larkin, who lifted a fly ball over the Braves' drawn-in outfield, bringing home the winning run and setting off a riot at home plate. The Twins were champs, and the celebration raged in the Metrodome.

Four years after their 1987 world championship, Puckett (above, center) led the Twins back to the top of the heap in 1991. He was the hero in Game 6, and Morris finished things with a clutch 10-inning shutout in the winner-take-all Game 7.

NEW YORK METS

THERE'S NO AVOIDING THE reality that the New York Mets, throughout certain portions of their history, have found ways to lose that boggled the mind. But in 1969, America was landing a man on the moon and the Miracle Mets were capturing one of Major League Baseball's most unlikely championships. New York controlled a stockpile of young talent that became the envy of baseball. Major contributors like shortstop Bud Harrelson, first baseman Ed Kranepool, outfielders Tommie Agee, Cleon Jones and Ron Swoboda, and pitchers Jerry Koosman, Gary Gentry and Nolan Ryan were all 26 or younger. So, too, was the franchise centerpiece, Tom Seaver. With Seaver winning the Cy Young Award and nearly the MVP trophy, skipper Gil Hodges' Mets dispatched the Orioles in five games to win the franchise's first world title.

The same nucleus won another pennant in 1973, only to sink into the basement later that decade. The bad years, though, resulted in high draft picks that were used to select the cornerstones of the next Mets juggernaut: Darryl Strawberry and Dwight Gooden. Management surrounded these two superstars with an incredible blend of talent, including 1979 NL MVP Keith Hernandez, Gary Carter, Ron Darling and Lenny Dykstra, and the turbocharged Mets won the 1986 championship one game after a ground ball famously bounced through Red Sox first baseman Bill Buckner's legs. The expected dynasty of that decade never quite materialized, but the Mets remained relevant for much of the next 20 years, winning a 1999 NLCS game on Robin Ventura's memorable "grand slam single" and battling the Yankees in the 2000 Subway Series.

With the Mets trailing the Red Sox, 3-2, in Game 6 of the 1986 Series, Carter — with an outfield assist from Mookie Wilson — nailed Jim Rice at home in the seventh inning to keep the game close.

to win their first title since 1918, but again they found themselves in a dogfight.

In Game 1 at Shea, Boston's Bruce Hurst and Calvin Schiraldi combined on a shutout. The next night was the real marquee matchup: Dwight Gooden against Roger Clemens. But the game was far from a pitchers' duel. The Sox jumped all over Gooden, pounding him and four Mets relievers for 18 hits in a 9-3 win. Clemens also struggled, failing to complete five innings.

Trailing in the Series, the Mets were faced with the prospect of playing three straight at Fenway Park. They managed to turn home-field advantage on its head, taking the third and fourth games, but Gooden came up short in Game 5, losing 4-2. Still, things weren't hopeless for the Mets: They could still clinch a championship by winning the next two games on their home turf.

In Game 6, a back-and-forth affair went to extra innings, and Boston took a 5-3 lead in the 10th. Down to their last out, it seemed like a sure bet that the Mets were done.

But then the unbelievable happened. A two-out rally cut the deficit to 5-4, and the tying run scored on a wild pitch. The Mets had life.

Ordinarily with a late-inning lead, the Red Sox would have removed its first baseman — Bill Buckner, playing injured — for a defensive replacement. But with the inning starting with the prospect of an on-field celebration, skipper John McNamara wanted to leave Buckner in the game. It was a fatal mistake. Mookie Wilson swung and hit a soft roller down the line that squeaked just underneath the glove and between the legs of the gimpy Buckner, scoring Ray Knight and winning the game for the Mets.

The dazed Red Sox tried to get back on their feet for Game 7, but their moment had passed. Although Boston took an early lead, New York stormed back with three runs in the sixth, three in the seventh and two in the eighth to put the game and the Series out of reach.

NOT 'TIL THE FAT LADY SINGS

Loaded with stars like Gooden, Hernandez and Lenny Dykstra (top), the Mets stormed back from the brink of elimination to win the 1986 Fall Classic.

New York ran roughshod over the NL East in 1986, posting 108 wins, the third-highest total in league history. As a result, the Mets entered October as the favorite, but they would encounter significant resistance along the way.

It began with the plucky NL West–champion Houston Astros. The Mets clinched the pennant by winning an epic 16-inning see-saw battle in Game 6 that left first baseman Keith Hernandez gushing, "This was the best league series ever."

The Mets were still the favorites heading into the World Series against the Boston Red Sox, who were trying

THE FRANCHISE

Although a moniker like "The Franchise" would suggest that a player was born with a presupposition for stardom, Tom Seaver had to work for everything he got. Far from the hardest thrower on his high school team, Seaver lifted weights and tirelessly refined his mechanics. He eventually built up his boyish frame while developing a devastating fastball and a deep reservoir of pitching knowledge.

Seaver arrived in Queens in 1966 after a dispute over the University of Southern California product's draft

Seaver (left) won three Cy Young Awards and the 1969 world title with the Mets. But while he may have been "The Franchise," it was the team's mascot that became known as Mr. Met.

rights jeopardized his NCAA eligibility. The Mets won Seaver in a strange lottery at the Commissioner's Office between three teams — the Cleveland Indians and Philadelphia Phillies included — that were bidding for his services. For New York, he proved a jackpot: an intelligent, hard-throwing, durable ace to take them to the top of the standings for the first time. In 1967, he won the NL Rookie of the Year Award with a 16-13 record. Two years later, during the team's magical ride to baseball heaven, Seaver won the Cy Young Award.

He faced each game's critical moments like a prizefighter in the boxing ring and was determined to win each confrontation. Although he was armed with a blistering fastball, Seaver preferred to out-think his foes, and thanks to such maturity and professionalism, he won consistently throughout his career (311 times total), even after a natural decline in arm strength.

On Aug. 4, 1985, he returned to New York as a 40-year-old member of the White Sox staff for a start against the Yankees in the Bronx. With 299 wins under his belt, Seaver was on the verge of joining the exclusive 300-win club, a mark he reached with a solid complete-game effort. It was the 228th complete game of his career, and he would add three more before his retirement the following season. In 1992, Seaver was voted into the Hall of Fame by 425 of the 430 voting writers.

During the club's most recent era, All-Star third baseman David Wright became the face of the Mets.

 Big Shots

18 **SEASONS** played in the Majors by Ed Kranepool. His four postseason Series with the team included a home run in the club's "miracle" win in 1969.

370 **STEALS** by Jose Reyes as a New York Met, setting a franchise record. The shortstop averaged 41 steals in nine seasons in New York.

108 **WINS** by the 1986 team on its way to a memorable World Series victory. The talented group led the league in runs (783) and won the East by 21.5 games.

26 **HOMERS** hit by Darryl Strawberry as a rookie Mets outfielder in 1983. The former top overall pick, he would finish with a team-record 252 blasts.

.337 **BATTING AVERAGE** posted by Reyes in 2011 to become the first Met ever to win the batting title.

3 **WINNING SEASONS** skippered by Gil Hodges (1969–71) in his four years at the helm. In 1962, the former Brooklyn hero also hit the Mets' first-ever home run.

MIRACLE

Tommy Agee (crossing home plate) led off the bottom of the first in Game 3 of the '69 World Series with a homer on the way to a 5-0 win. Pitcher Jerry Koosman leapt into Jerry Grote's arms after the Series' last out was made.

Prior to 1969, the Mets were beloved losers. Despite winning over plenty of fans, they had lost 120, 111, 109, 112, 95 and 101 games in their first six seasons before improving to 73-89 in 1968. The hapless Mets featured luminaries such as "Marvelous" Marv Throneberry, a first baseman famous mostly for his ineptitude — and for being the only player in franchise history with the initials M.E.T.

Throughout the '60s, though, the Mets were gradually assembling the foundation of a solid team, and in '69 everything came together. Their strength was their pitching staff. Tom Seaver, at age 24, came of age in spectacular fashion that year, going 25-7 with a 2.21 ERA and 18 complete games. He easily won the NL Cy Young Award, and narrowly missed winning the MVP Award.

On Aug. 15, the Mets were in third, 10 games behind first-place Chicago. But over the next month, New York went 27-7 to win the division, and kept its momentum by sweeping Atlanta in the NLCS, setting up a World Series matchup with the heavily favored Orioles.

The seemingly invincible Seaver lost the first game to Baltimore, and it looked like the rout was on. But Koosman evened things up for the Mets in Game 2, hurling a two-hitter. Games 3 and 4, the first World Series contests ever played at Shea Stadium, were close matchups that went in the Mets' favor, thanks to some stellar fielding.

Just one win away from their first title, the Mets fell behind, 3-0, in Game 5. In the bottom of the sixth, though, New York's Donn Clendenon hit a two-run homer, and in the seventh, Al Weis — who had just seven homers in 10

seasons — hit a game-tying bomb to left field. The Mets' comeback was capped by Ron Swoboda's double in the eighth. An inning later, Jones caught the fly ball that ended what remains one of baseball's greatest storybook seasons.

THE CATCH

It was "a superman catch," David Wright told the New York *Daily News* of Endy Chavez's leaping grab at the left–center field fence during Game 7 of the 2006 NLCS. Considering the situation (one on, one out, 1-1 score in the sixth inning with the season on the line), it was also one of the best plays in the 45-year history of Shea Stadium, even if New York did ultimately lose the game, 3-1.

The drive by St. Louis third baseman Scott Rolen seemed a sure home run off the bat. But Chavez sprinted back to the warning track and left his feet, pulling the ball back from beyond the wall with the tip of his glove. "I thought I had no chance, because the ball was far from me," Chavez told the *Daily News*. "I tried to jump as high as I could. My glove almost came off my hand. I wanted to keep it inside my glove. I had to check for it."

Chavez's spectacular grab was one of many highlights for the '06 Mets, a healthy mix of emerging stars and proven veterans that combined to post a league-best 97-65 record. From 23-year-olds Wright and Jose Reyes to 47-year-old Julio Franco — and everyone in between — the Mets packed an offensive punch, as well as one of the best bullpens in the league, anchored by southpaw Billy Wagner.

"I THOUGHT I HAD NO CHANCE. MY GLOVE ALMOST CAME OFF. I HAD TO CHECK FOR THE BALL."
—ENDY CHAVEZ

NEW YORK YANKEES

THE YANKEES ARE NOT ONLY THE most accomplished franchise in baseball history, but they also have as many championships — 27 — as any three teams combined. It all started in 1920, when the Yankees snookered the Red Sox out of Babe Ruth in return for $125,000. After that, the baseball world would never be the same.

Ruth's Yankees won three consecutive AL pennants from 1921–23, but it wasn't until Lou Gehrig joined the lineup full time in 1925 that the Yankees truly became the *Yankees*. Ruth and Gehrig won three championships together, and the Iron Horse bagged three more after Ruth's retirement.

In 1941 the Yankees celebrated America's last pre-war summer with Joe DiMaggio's 56-game hitting streak and, of course, another title. By 1996, though, the club had gone 17 years without a ring, its longest drought since the pre-Ruth era. Like they did with Casey Stengel in 1949, the Yankees made waves by hiring a veteran manager with a losing career record, and once again the move was a smashing success. Joe Torre's extraordinary calm was the heartbeat at the center of these new Bronx Bombers, and with the quintet of Derek Jeter, Mariano Rivera, Bernie Williams, Jorge Posada and Andy Pettitte leading the way, New York won four championships and averaged 98 wins per season during Torre's tenure. That same core — minus Williams, whose final year came in 2006 — claimed the title once more in 2009, with a six-game triumph over the defending champion Phillies. The formula is simple: In New York, the Yankees are synonymous with winning, and nothing but the best will suffice.

SULTAN OF SWAT

It's hard to believe that before the trade that sent Ruth to New York, the club had next to no record of success. By the time he left town, the Yankees had become the team that all others would forvever be judged against.

The year was 1920, and Yankees scholars agree that it was a sea-change moment in the franchise's — and the sport's — history. That was the season Babe Ruth arrived in New York, ready to reshape the way the Yankees scored runs and, more to the point, how America came to appreciate baseball. Ruth didn't just edge out his historical competitors; he lapped the field several times over. He broke the home run record (a mark he had set just the previous year) with his 30th roundtripper on July 19, 1920, more than two months before the end of the season. His final total of 54 home runs was more than any *team* had hit in five years. To those who had never seen anything even remotely like it, Ruth was a revelation, more force of nature than baseball player.

Famously, for a mere $125,000, plus a $300,000 loan, the greatest he-man baseball would ever know was traded from Boston to New York.

For modern fans, it's perhaps difficult to comprehend just how drastically Ruth transformed the game. In 1913, the year before Ruth's debut with Boston, the entire Yankees team combined to hit eight homers. In 1920, Ruth hit eight in a week. Ruth broke the single-season home run record four times. He out-slugged entire teams on a routine basis. He batted as high as .393, drove in as many as 171 runs and crossed the plate as many as 177 times in a single season. He was so popular upon arriving in New York that the Yankees began to outdraw the Giants, in whose stadium the Yanks played. Thus, the Giants ownership forced the tenants out of their ballpark, paving the way for the Yankees to build a stadium in the Bronx that — with its short right-field porch — was tailor-made for Ruth.

At age 32, Ruth finally reached his peak, hitting 60 home runs — a record that would stand until 1961 — while amassing 164 RBI. That was Ruth's final brush with greatness, though, as the younger and better conditioned Lou Gehrig soon became the hub of the Bronx Bombers' offense. But only one Yankee could ever say he built a stadium — or, more precisely, only one Yankee ever had a stadium built for him.

Jeter reached 3,000 in typically legendary fashion, putting together a 5-for-5 day and homering off Rays ace David Price for the monumental hit. He's just the second member of the esteemed club to earn membership with a longball.

CAPTAIN CLUTCH

Heading into 2011, the baseball world had little doubt about one thing: By season's end, a revered milestone would be reached, and Derek Jeter would be the newest player — and the first Yankee — to notch his 3,000th hit.

The 3,000-hit club is noteworthy in large part for the players who *failed* to join. The elite list doesn't include Babe Ruth, whose hits totals suffered from his high walk rate. Others absent from the club include Ted Williams, who also walked often and missed several years serving in the military, and Lou Gehrig, whose career ended early due to a terminal illness. Rogers Hornsby, Barry Bonds,

Frank Robinson, Mel Ott, Jimmie Foxx and Joe DiMaggio are among baseball's other shining stars who fell short, but after passing the 2,900-hit mark in September 2010 and concluding the year perched at 2,926, Jeter stood in perfect position to join the 3,000-hit ranks in 2011.

With all of the national attention on Jeter and his pursuit of the milestone, the Yankees' captain could not have found a more dramatic way to reach the mark. Facing tough Rays lefty David Price on July 9, Jeter crushed a fastball to the left-field seats for his 3,000th hit, part of a 5-for-5 day. He became just the second member of the elite club to reach the mark on a home run, after Wade Boggs did so in 1999.

Jackson's three homers in Game 6 of the 1977 World Series made the "Mr. October" nickname stick.

Yankees Hall of Famers

YOGI BERRA
Won three MVP Awards.

JACK CHESBRO
Recorded a 1.82 ERA in 1904.

EARLE COMBS
A career .325 hitter.

BILL DICKEY
An 11-time All-Star and a durable backstop.

JOE DiMAGGIO
Won three MVP Awards.

WHITEY FORD
Won a record 10 World Series decisions.

LOU GEHRIG
Recorded 184 RBI in 1931.

LEFTY GOMEZ
Won 20 games four times.

JOE GORDON
A nine-time All-Star and the 1942 AL MVP.

RICH GOSSAGE
Tallied 124 wins and 310 saves.

WAITE HOYT
Allowed zero earned runs in 27 innings in the 1921 Series.

REGGIE JACKSON
Slugged 563 career homers.

WILLIE KEELER
Posted a .341 average in 19 seasons.

TONY LAZZERI
Played clutch defense at second base.

MICKEY MANTLE
Most career homers by a switch-hitter (536).

HERB PENNOCK
Won 241 games.

PHIL RIZZUTO
Recorded 200 hits in 1950, when he won the MVP Award.

RED RUFFING
Won 273 career games on the mound.

Arguably the greatest switch-hitter of all time, Mantle's name is still all over the postseason record books. He had plenty of chances to build his resume, playing in 12 World Series during his 18-year career.

AMERICAN IDOL

In one 16-year period, from 1949 through '64, one team won 14 pennants and nine World Series. That team was, of course, the New York Yankees, and the dominant player on that team, from his arrival in the Big Leagues in 1951 through the 1964 season, was Mickey Mantle.

The first World Series Mantle ever took part in was during his rookie season. While that 1951 Fall Classic would be the first of many magnificent Octobers for No. 7, it also saw his career start down a path dogged by repeated injuries. In Game 2 at Yankee Stadium, Mantle stepped on a water sprinkler in right field trying to make a catch and blew out his knee. He suffered another World Series injury in 1957, when the Yankees faced the Milwaukee Braves. As Mantle dove back to second base on an attempted pick-off, Braves second baseman Red Schoendienst landed on the Mick's right shoulder. Many

believe the great switch-hitter never fully recovered his power from the left side.

But the Mickey Mantle World Series story was one more of triumph than disappointment. In his second Series, in 1952 against the Brooklyn Dodgers, his homer in Game 6 provided the winning margin for the Yankees, while another homer in Game 7 put his team ahead to stay. In 1956, he preserved Don Larsen's perfect game with a catch in center field that he and others considered the best of his career.

Mantle left behind an unforgettable — and unsurpassed — record of World Series greatness. Nearly five decades later, the Mick still pervades the World Series record book like no other player. He holds the career Fall Classic records for home runs, RBI, runs scored, total bases and walks. And he ranks second only to teammate Yogi Berra in World Series games played, at-bats and hits.

THE CLIPPER

It was during 13 magical All-Star seasons with the power-house New York Yankees, from the mid-1930s to the start of the 1950s, that Joe DiMaggio's legend cemented itself in America's consciousness. With Joe D leading the way, both as a graceful center fielder and a menace with a bat in his hands, the team won 10 American League pennants and nine World Series crowns in 13 years, including titles in his first four years with the team.

DiMaggio's many individual accomplishments are legendary — three Most Valuable Player Awards, two batting crowns and a 56-game hitting streak that may go down in history as the sport's most untouchable record — and those who got to see him play in those halcyon days referred to him in reverential terms.

Despite missing almost half of the 1934 campaign with the San Francisco Seals of the Pacific Coast League due to a knee injury, the Yankees had faith in DiMaggio's future. New York purchased him from San Francisco for $25,000 and five players, with the understanding that he would remain with the Seals for the 1935 season.

With Babe Ruth having retired and Lou Gehrig nearing the end of his playing days, the Yankees were putting their faith in a young player who had never seen a pitch in the Major Leagues, but DiMaggio burst onto the sporting landscape like few others, finishing his first season in Yankees pinstripes with 29 homers, 125 RBI, 132 runs scored and a .323 average.

Despite serving his country in the armed forces for three seasons during his prime — from 1943–45, between the ages of 28 and 30 — DiMaggio still amassed 361 career homers and 881 total extra-base hits. Fittingly, given his outstanding production in the 13 seasons he did play, not to mention the high regard among fans, media and fellow ballplayers, DiMaggio was elected to the Hall of Fame without pause in 1955. He remains to this day one of the greatest center fielders the game has ever known.

Those who saw DiMaggio in action insist that no one ever played the game quite like he did. Had he not missed three years in his prime due to World War II, Joe D's career numbers would certainly inspire even more acclaim.

GREATEST OF ALL TIME

Teammates and opponents alike agree that when it comes to imposing forces on the mound, Mariano Rivera is as good as it gets.

The resident pinstriped closer garnered even more reason for praise on Sept. 17, 2011, when he notched his 600th save in a win against the Mariners at Safeco Field, and again six days later, when he passed Trevor Hoffman with his 602nd — which came at home against the Minnesota Twins — to claim the all-time record.

In more than 15 years with the Yankees, Rivera joined a list of just 15 people who have appeared in more than 1,000 games, and he averaged 40 saves a season since taking over the closer's job full time in 1997. He also became a regular at the Midsummer Classic and won the World Series MVP Award in 1999.

Much like Hoffman, his 600-saves-club predecessor, Rivera does the vast majority of his damage with one signature pitch: a cut fastball.

Although hitters always knew what to expect with No. 42 on the mound, it wasn't any easier for them to hit him. Rivera spent most of his later years as the ERA leader for active pitchers, hovering near 2.20.

Really, no doubt remains that Rivera is the game's greatest shutdown reliever; the best there is or ever was. Every single save, from one through 600 and beyond, is a notch on the belt of a timeless arm, a relief pitcher whose skill knows no age and whose legacy is glory-bound for Cooperstown.

 *Stripes*

114 **WINS** by Joe Torre's 1998 Yankees, a franchise record. Led by a bevy of homegrown talent, New York dominated the American League East, winning the division by 22 games.

41 **WINS** reached by spitballer Jack Chesbro for the 1904 New York Highlanders (as the Yankees were then known). The 30-year-old Chesbro also completed 48 games that year.

0.77 **ERA** recorded by closer Mariano Rivera in his first 76 postseason appearances, a span of 117.1 innings pitched. Understandably, Rivera is considered by most baseball experts to be the greatest closer of all time, particularly in the postseason.

3 **HOME RUNS** smacked by Reggie Jackson on three consecutive pitches in the 1977 World Series to help the Yankees top the Dodgers in Game 6.

142 **RBI** put up by right fielder Roger Maris in 1961 during his record-breaking 61-homer season. During that same campaign, his teammate Mickey Mantle belted 54 and knocked in 128 of his own. Maris came away with the American League Most Valuable Player Award.

.440 **ON-BASE PERCENTAGE** posted by Joe DiMaggio in 1941, his famed 56-game-hit-streak season. In 541 at-bats that year, Joe D struck out just 13 times.

The "Core Four" — (from left) Jorge Posada, Rivera, Derek Jeter and Andy Pettitte — won five world titles together and, in 2008, closed down the House That Ruth Built for good, leading the team across the street to a new ballpark.

OAKLAND ATHLETICS

DESPITE ENDURING FINANCIAL hardship in each of the three cities that the franchise has called home, the Oakland Athletics have not only persevered, but thrived. They won more championships — nine — in the 20th century than all but two other franchises. In each of their three homes, the A's have been successful under the direction of a forward-thinking member of management.

Derided as "white elephants" by Giants Manager John McGraw after Benjamin Shibe bought the controlling interest of the team in 1901, the defiant A's adopted the pachyderm as their logo and won six pennants and three World Series during the AL's first 14 years. Second baseman Eddie Collins was arguably the league's finest player during that era, while Frank Baker earned the nickname "Home Run" after slugging the then–*Philadelphia* A's to the 1911 title. In the late '20s and early '30s, a second great dynasty developed, this one led by pitcher Lefty Grove, catcher Mickey Cochrane and slugger Jimmie Foxx.

After a move to Kansas City in 1955, the club struggled and ultimately never was able to make things work in the Midwest, despite innovative thinking from Owner Charlie Finley, who invested heavily in the farm system for the first time in the franchise's history. In 1968, Finley relocated his club to the West Coast, where Catfish Hunter pitched a perfect game in just the 11th contest ever played in Oakland. The A's then rolled to three straight championship seasons from 1972–74.

Oakland won again in 1989, the year Billy Beane joined the organization as an outfielder. After his playing days, the disciple of baseball historian and statistician Bill James moved up the ranks until he was named GM in 1997, and sparked a baseball revolution by popularizing the use of sabermetrics in decision-making. Beane's methods helped the A's reach the playoffs five times on a tight budget in the 2000s and, with the release of the film *Moneyball*, gave Brad Pitt the source material for an Oscar–nominated performance.

THE OLD GUARD

Mack's (left) A's tenure lasted half a century, as the manager led the club to nine pennants and five championships. Foxx, meanwhile, was one of the club's best players even during his first season as a regular starter at age 20.

After joining the Philadelphia A's at age 17, Jimmie Foxx lingered on the bench for three seasons while learning the game from Connie Mack, Ty Cobb, Tris Speaker and Eddie Collins — perhaps the four savviest men in baseball at the time. When Foxx turned 20, his apprenticeship was declared over, and he proceeded to hit at least 30 home runs and drive in 100 or more runs for 12 consecutive seasons, a Major League record. His best season came in 1932, when he batted .364, made a run at Ruth's single-season record with 58 longballs and drove in 169 runs.

Under Mack's wise leadership, the A's won back-to-back world championships in 1929 and '30, and they added an American League pennant in 1931. Perhaps the finest of these teams was the 1929 squad, which won 104 regular-season games and the World Series. The team hit .296 that year, with Foxx posting a .463 on-base percentage. The pitching was just as strong, with two 20-game winners in Lefty Grove and George Earnshaw. The rotation was so deep that the A's didn't even start Grove in the Fall Classic, despite his Major League–leading 2.81 ERA.

Midway through his career, Foxx seemed destined to become the all-time home run leader; 700 or even 800 homers were well within his reach. He became the youngest player ever to reach 300 homers (27 years, 328 days), 400 homers (30 years, 248 days) and 500 homers (32 years, 338 days). The first two marks were broken by both Ken Griffey Jr. and Alex Rodriguez, and A-Rod also broke the latter record. But by the time Foxx reached his early 30s, chronic alcoholism and poor conditioning had taken their toll. He hit just 15 home runs after the age of 33, by far the fewest of any member of the 500 home run club.

Mack, for his part, enjoyed a great deal of success in his 30s … and 40s and 50s and well up into his 80s. As a player-manager with the Pirates for three seasons from 1894–96, Mack didn't reach the playoffs despite records above .500. After he became a full-time manager in 1901, though, Mack would manage for 50 years, winning five World Series and another four AL pennants. When he finally stepped down — at the remarkable age of 87 — his 3,731 managerial wins were far and away the most in baseball history. The only manager within 1,000 wins is John McGraw, a distant 968 behind.

BATTLE BY THE BAY

For reporters assigned to cover the 1989 World Series between the San Francisco Giants and the Oakland A's, the who, what, where and why were easy. It was the when that was causing problems. When would the Battle of the Bay resume? No one had an answer after a 7.1-magnitude earthquake that struck just moments before Game 3 devastated Northern California.

The quake was centered in Loma Prieta, about 60 miles south of the Giants' home in Candlestick Park, but it was felt throughout the Bay Area. Led by Oakland native and A's ace Dave Stewart — who went 21-9 with a 3.32 ERA in the regular season and 4-0 with a 2.25 ERA in the postseason, eventually finishing second in Cy Young voting — some players spent part of the 10-day layoff helping with relief efforts.

When all was said and done, the longest World Series in baseball history went just four games. The A's — with a two-game lead heading to San Francisco — went on to win Games 3 and 4 by scores of 13-7 and 9-6, respectively, completing the sweep. Aside from a scoreless tie at the end of the first inning of the Series, Oakland led every frame except for one. Stewart, with two victories and a 1.69 ERA, was named World Series MVP, but A's closer Dennis Eckersley — who saved 33 games in the regular season and posted a 1.56 ERA — also pitched superbly in the postseason, saving four games and giving up just one run in 7.1 innings. The A's decided against a raucous post-game clubhouse celebration, choosing instead to host a party for the players and their families. Even after one of history's most decisive routs, no one was in the mood to celebrate.

Stewart said the goal in that Series was not to separate the A's from the Giants, but to unite Oakland and San Francisco. "In a funny way, I think the earthquake was good for the Bay, both sides," Stewart said afterward. "It's always been said we are separated by water, and that wasn't the only thing. We were two totally different sides, but after the earthquake, two sides came together to turn something that was bad — a tragedy — into something good."

Despite Oakland's on-field celebration after winning the 1989 Fall Classic (above), the mood in the Bay Area was somber in the wake of the earthquake. Stewart wasn't fazed by the chaos, going 2-0 on his way to the Series MVP Award.

A's lefty Dallas Braden tossed a perfect game against the Tampa Bay Rays on May 9, 2010, in Oakland. He struck out six batters on the day.

Enter Billy Beane, who was named GM in 1998. Beane armed himself with a front office — including Paul DePodesta, who then served as his assistant — that took an alternate approach to building a roster. He used sabermetric statistical analysis to evaluate players and focused on attributes that were typically undervalued in the market, such as the ability to draw walks. The result in '02 was a team that won 102 games — including 20 in a row from mid-August to early September — and claimed the AL West title. The team batted .299 with 30 homers during the streak, and the pitching staff posted a 2.65 ERA as the A's rebounded from a 20-26 start.

Although they would ultimately fall in the playoffs, the 2002 Athletics remain a testament to the power of Beane's vision and philosophy, one that still permeates the game today.

Beane and the A's front office sparked a revolution that changed the way baseball players are analyzed today. His practices were documented in the book *Moneyball*, which was turned into a film in 2011.

JACKPOT

It was 2002, the prime of what would come to be known as the "Moneyball" era. The Oakland Athletics, who had always competed against big spenders like the Yankees in the American League, had to find a way of creating a contending team without breaking the bank to sign any superstar free agents.

RUNNING RICKEY

The axiom may be as old as baseball itself: You can't steal first base. Rickey Henderson, however, could steal the opposing team's thunder, not to mention second and third. Irrepressible, sometimes unbelievable, Henderson had a knack for getting on the nerves of managers, his own as well as his opponents.

Henderson didn't exactly revolutionize baseball. There had been plenty of dynamic base stealers before him — although none who could hit with the same level of power — but he added a different dimension, an aggression that kept everyone off balance.

The essence of baseball is to prevent the other team from crossing home plate — and yes, no one denies the

Athletics Hall of Famers

FRANK BAKER . . . . "Home Run" Baker led the league in homers in four straight years from 1911–14.
CHARLES ALBERT BENDER . "Chief" Bender led AL pitchers in winning percentage three times.
MICKEY COCHRANE . . . . Hit at a .320 career clip and served as a leader from behind the plate.
DENNIS ECKERSLEY . . . . Won the AL MVP and Cy Young awards in 1992.
ROLLIE FINGERS . . . . Posted a 2.90 career ERA, pitching primarily as a top-notch reliever.
RICKEY HENDERSON . . . . . . Holds the all-time career stolen base record by a substantial margin with 1,406.
CATFISH HUNTER . . . . Won 20-plus games five straight times.
EDDIE PLANK . . . . Won 326 games, third all time for a lefty.
AL SIMMONS . . . . Hit at a .334 clip with 1,827 RBI in his 20 seasons.
RUBE WADDELL . . . . The eccentric southpaw led the AL in strikeouts six straight times.

Henderson, who grew up in Oakland, went on to a decorated career in his hometown. The speedy outfielder — and eventual Hall of Famer — appropriately earned the nickname "Man of Steal" and owns the career record for stolen bases.

importance of pitching and defense — while getting your own men to reach home safely. For the second part of the equation, Henderson could not be equaled.

In 1982, on an August evening in Milwaukee, Henderson broke one of the game's most cherished records by stealing his 119th, 120th, 121st and 122nd bases, surpassing the single-season mark of 118 set by Lou Brock in 1974. Rickey would end up with 130 on the season, and would eventually finish with a record 1,406 for his 25-year career.

Henderson was born in Chicago on Christmas Day 1958, but he grew up in Oakland and became a football and baseball star at Oakland Technical High. Thus it was perfect that in 1991, when he broke Brock's career mark of 938 stolen bases, he was wearing the A's gold and green and playing a home game in the city where he used to outrun buses down the streets as a kid.

He stayed on the move during his career, both on the field and among the nine different teams for which he played. Running Rickey. Misunderstood Rickey. Yes, he celebrated that 939th steal by hoisting the bag at Oakland-Alameda County Coliseum and declaring, "I am the greatest of all time," but that was taken out of context from a speech Brock himself helped Henderson compose.

Rickey was the ALCS MVP in 1989 before batting .474 in the A's sweep of the Giants in the earthquake-marred World Series. He followed that up by winning the AL MVP Award in 1990.

So many numbers: The 3,055 hits, the 2,295 runs, the 2,190 walks, the 81 leadoff home runs and the 20 or more dingers in four different seasons. Asked if Rickey, who served as a coach with the Mets in 2007, was a Hall of Famer, the statistician Bill James declared, "If you split him in two, you'd have two Hall of Famers."

PHILADELPHIA PHILLIES

F OR MOST OF A CENTURY, THE Philadelphia Phillies endured a frustrating futility that made them the last of the 16 "original" Major League teams to win a World Series. But in 1971, the Phils drafted arguably the greatest third baseman ever — Mike Schmidt — and the franchise reversed course dramatically, becoming a consistent winner. In the nearly four decades since Schmidt became a regular in 1974, Philadelphia has posted a winning percentage higher than .500 and won more than 3,000 games, two of the best marks in Major League Baseball.

Philly's early home at the Baker Bowl was a hitter's paradise, especially during the raucous 1890s, when the lineup featured three Hall of Famers in the same outfield. In 1894, Billy Hamilton's .403 batting average was the *worst* in the Phillies outfield. It would take a great pitcher, though, to finally carry Philadelphia to its first pennant. Pete Alexander hurled the Phils to the 1915 flag on the strength of 31 wins and a 1.22 ERA, both of which led MLB. Another memorable pennant followed in 1950, when a group of fresh-faced youngsters dubbed the "Whiz Kids" edged out Brooklyn on the season's final day.

In the 1970s and '80s Schmidt dominated the Majors with an all-around game that included eight home run titles, a .380 lifetime on-base percentage and 10 Gold Gloves. Aided by southpaw Steve Carlton and a stellar supporting cast, Schmidt led the Phillies to five NL East titles and the 1980 world championship — the franchise's first. A brief lull after winning the 1993 NL pennant ended during the 2000s, when a crew led by Chase Utley, Ryan Howard and Jimmy Rollins arrived on the scene. That trio of homegrown stars helped the Phils capture five more division crowns from 2007–11, as well as the 2008 World Series title.

Roy Halladay and catcher Carlos Ruiz embraced after Doc completed his no-hitter against the Cincinnati Reds in Game 1 of the 2010 NLDS.

THE HOT CORNER

Mike Schmidt finally seemed at ease. It was 1982, the third baseman's 10th season with the Phillies, and the weight of expectations appeared lifted from his broad shoulders. "The level I play the game at now is one that not many players have played it at," Schmidt admitted during Spring Training.

Few could argue. His first seven seasons had been well above average, but he had elevated his game to another stratosphere by 1982, having won back-to-back MVP Awards in 1980 and '81 (and a World Series ring in '80). Schmidt led the league in OPS and RBI in both seasons, which went along with Gold Glove defense.

"Mike was the best player in the league three or four days a week when I got there," said ex-teammate Pete Rose, who arrived in Philly in 1979. "By the time I left [in 1984], he had learned to be the best seven days a week."

Of those who spent at least 80 percent of their time in the field at the hot corner, Schmidt leads them all in home runs, RBI and OPS+, and is third in runs scored. He accumulated all of these impressive figures as a member of the Phillies, to boot.

Schmidt added a third MVP Award in 1986. Three years later, he wrapped up arguably the greatest career ever by a third baseman. That his hometown fans had occasionally (and infamously) booed him was no black mark on his record. "The man's only crime," wrote Dave Kindred after Schmidt retired, "was to come to the ballpark with a gift so large he made hard things look easy."

AT LONG LAST

In 2007 the Phillies became the first Major League franchise in history to lose 10,000 games. Founded in 1883, the organization boasted just one World Series title since the Fall Classic's inception in 1903.

And yet, at 8:38 p.m. on Oct. 22, 2008, Tampa Bay Rays left-hander Scott Kazmir threw the first pitch of one of the most unlikely World Series matchups in Big League history. Seven nights later, the Phillies were world champions.

The games held sway over fans, who got much enjoyment from the tight matchups that the Series had to offer;

Schmidt, who spent his entire 18-year career with the Phillies, has a strong case for being the best third baseman in history after winning three MVP Awards and 10 Gold Glove Awards.

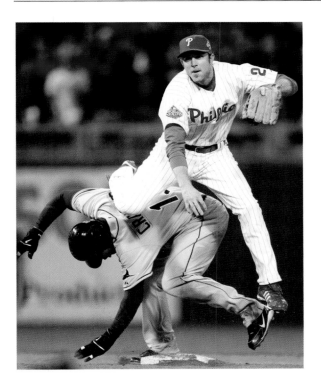

things like four of the five games being decided by a combined five runs. It saw Game 5 begin on Oct. 27 with the Phillies on the brink of a clinch; and end at 9:58 p.m. on Oct. 29, nearly 50 hours later, thanks to a rainstorm in Philly. And in the end, it saw a city that hadn't celebrated any major sports title since 1983 explode into euphoria.

Two players in particular, Geoff Jenkins and Pat Burrell, made the most of their lone Series hits. When Game 5 resumed in the bottom of the sixth inning, Jenkins led off with a double off the wall in right-center field. He scored on a Jayson Werth bloop hit, but the Rays tied it in the seventh on a Rocco Baldelli homer. Leading off the bottom of that inning, Burrell strode to the plate, 0 for 13 in the Fall Classic to that point. But he was about to make his one hit count. He cranked lefty J.P. Howell's curveball to the top of the wall in center field for a double. Eric Bruntlett pinch-ran and scored the Series' winning run on a Pedro Feliz single.

From there it was just a tense waiting game until closer Brad Lidge came in to finish the job. And once he got Eric Hinske swinging to end it, the Phillies and their fans got to enjoy a celebration a quarter-century — and two rain-soaked days — in the making.

Despite Carl Crawford's attempt to take out Chase Utley in the eighth inning of Game 5 in the '08 Series (left), the second base-man successfully turned two, which led to a celebration later that night.

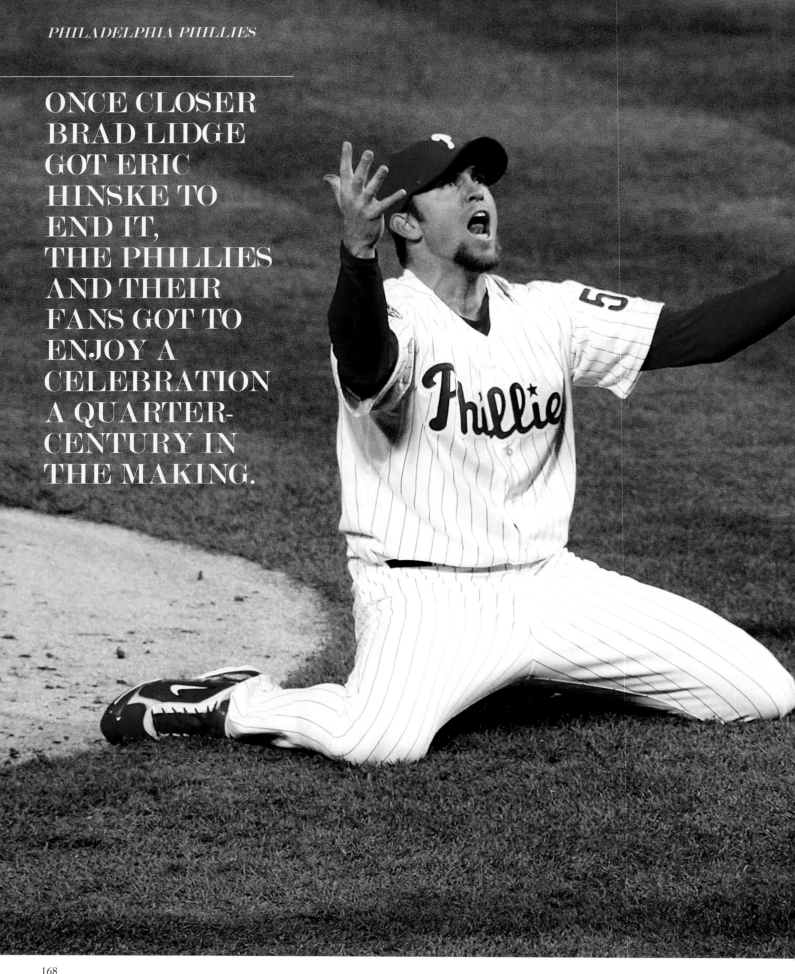

ONCE CLOSER BRAD LIDGE GOT ERIC HINSKE TO END IT, THE PHILLIES AND THEIR FANS GOT TO ENJOY A CELEBRATION A QUARTER-CENTURY IN THE MAKING.

DOC'S NO-NO

Halladay needed just 104 pitches to toss a no-hitter against the Reds in Game 1 of the 2010 NLDS, his first career playoff start. He finished with eight K's and faced one batter over the minimum.

Phillies right-hander Roy Halladay saved his best for *first*. Making his first career postseason start — after 11 seasons in which his former team, the Toronto Blue Jays, finished out of contention in the AL East — Halladay took the mound in Game 1 of the 2010 National League Division Series against Cincinnati with his usual tenacity and focus. What he produced was a start for the ages, something the likes of which hadn't been seen since Don Larsen twirled perfection in 1956.

Against the Reds, who had led or were near the top of many offensive categories in the National League in 2010, Halladay looked almost effortlessly effective, setting down the first 14 men who came to the plate. It wasn't until Jay Bruce drew a two-out, full-count walk in the fifth that the Reds sniffed the bases, and they wouldn't again afterward.

Boasting his signature five-pitch arsenal and deftly using it to paint the corners and miss bats — Reds hitters swung and missed 19 times — Doc masterfully made history after retiring Brandon Phillips on a weak grounder

Phillies Hall of Famers

GROVER CLEVELAND "PETE" ALEXANDER
Won 373 total games.

RICHIE ASHBURN
Batted .308 and had 2,574 base hits over a career spent mostly in the leadoff spot.

DAVE BANCROFT
Played stellar defense at shortstop and hit .294 in the 1915 World Series for the Phillies.

JIM BUNNING
Won 100 games and whiffed 1,000 batters in both the American and National Leagues before going on to become a U.S. senator.

STEVE CARLTON
Won 329 games and four Cy Young Awards.

ED DELAHANTY
Hit .400 three times and .346 overall.

BILLY HAMILTON
Swiped 914 total bases and batted .300 or better in 12 consecutive seasons.

CHUCK KLEIN
Won the 1933 National League Triple Crown with .368-28-120 totals one season after winning the NL MVP Award.

ROBIN ROBERTS
Rarely missed a start and won 20 games in six straight seasons.

MIKE SCHMIDT
Mashed 548 home runs and played Gold Glove–caliber defense at third base.

SAM THOMPSON
Put up a stellar .331 career average.

At just 23 years old, Hall of Fame–bound right-hander Roberts helped the 1950 "Whiz Kids" win the franchise's second National League pennant by recording a 3.02 ERA and winning 20 games, five of which were shutouts.

to catcher Carlos Ruiz. He became the second pitcher ever to throw a no-hitter in the playoffs, separated from Larsen's perfection by that lone walk to Bruce. In all, Halladay struck out eight Reds en route to his no-no. For good measure, he even added a two-out RBI single in the second inning. It was a night that completely belonged to Doc, a historic performance whose images are sure to live on in Citizens Bank Park for generations.

WHIZ KIDS

Sportswriter Harry Grayson picked the Phillies to win the pennant in 1950 and began calling the club the "Whiz Kids." It's not entirely certain if Grayson was referring to the team's overall youth or playing off the term *Quiz Kids*, the name of a 1940s radio program.

Regardless of the catchy nickname or the impression of one baseball writer, Philadelphia fans needed some

convincing in light of the franchise's dismal history: The Phillies had been a perennial second-division club, finishing in the bottom half of the division all but two years dating back to 1918 and in last place a staggering 16 times between 1919 and 1945.

But Manager Eddie Sawyer ran the team with a steady hand, and the Phils thrived thanks to a balanced lineup and the strong 1-2 pitching combo of Robin Roberts and Curt Simmons. They built a 7.5-game lead in mid-September and survived a late run of injuries entering a showdown with Jackie Robinson, Duke Snider and 35,073 raucous Brooklyn Dodgers fans that packed Ebbets Field for the season finale, which Philly won, 4-1.

Even though the Phillies were swept by the Yankees in that year's World Series, the "Whiz Kids" had won the hearts of a skeptical fan base with their unity and hustle.

"The best thing about that season was the camaraderie we had," said catcher Andy Seminick. "It was just one of those teams where everyone got along. It was like we were all brothers."

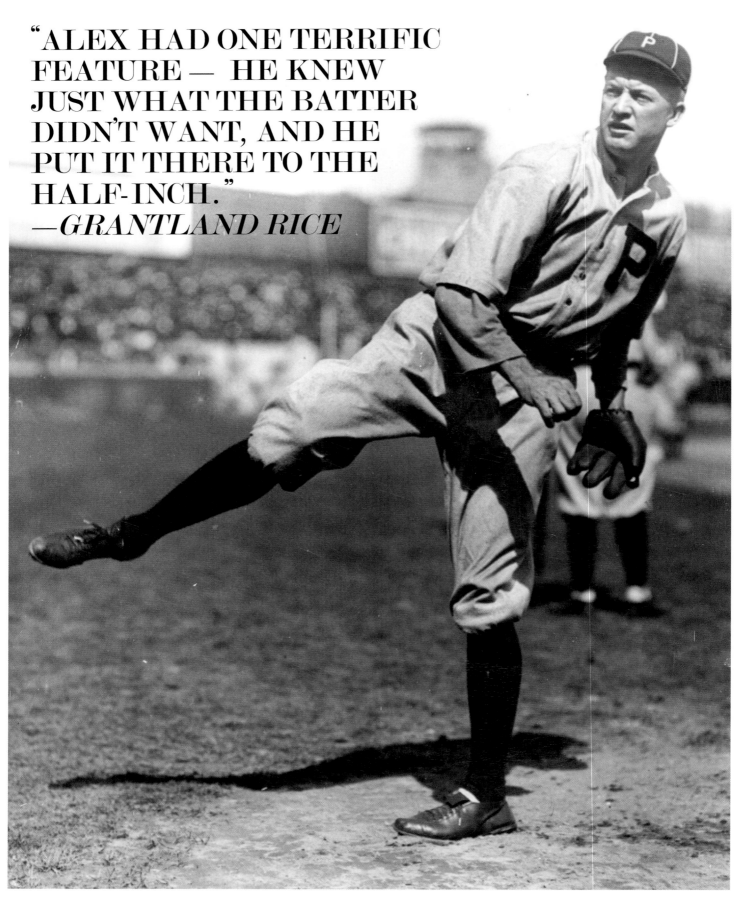

"ALEX HAD ONE TERRIFIC FEATURE — HE KNEW JUST WHAT THE BATTER DIDN'T WANT, AND HE PUT IT THERE TO THE HALF-INCH."
—*GRANTLAND RICE*

The Phillies and the Colorado Rockies lined up prior to Game 1 of the 2007 NLDS, which marked the Phils' first postseason trip in 14 years.

EFFORTLESS

A rawboned right-handed hurler straight off a Nebraska farm, Grover Cleveland "Pete" Alexander broke into the Majors with a flourish in 1911, setting a modern rookie record with 28 wins. Using a wide variety of breaking pitches, deceptive speed and pinpoint control, the Phillies' hurler soon found himself being compared to the top pitchers of his era.

His years with the Phillies were great ones. From 1911–17, Alexander took the mound 329 times, including 277 starts, tossing a grand total of 2,492 innings with a 2.12 ERA. Even in a pitching-dominated era, that mark was a cut above the rest. Alexander also led the National League in strikeouts in five of his seven years in the City of Brotherly Love, and was one of just eight pitchers to top 200 strikeouts in a season during that time. Only the legendary Walter Johnson did that more frequently during Alexander's time in Philadelphia.

Alexander would end his career in 1930 with 373 wins, still the third most in Major League history, as well as a boatload of other records. Upon Alexander's death in 1950, famed sportswriter Grantland Rice penned that he was the most cunning, the smartest and the best control pitcher baseball had ever seen, adding, "Above everything else, Alex had one terrific feature to his pitching — he knew just what the batter didn't want, and he put it there to the half-inch."

Fellow Hall of Fame pitcher Carl Hubbell may have summed up Alexander's complicated life and battle with alcoholism best when he said, "If Alex had taken care of himself he might have pitched until he was 50, because even when he was working in a game, he looked as though he was just warming up."

P Phacts and Phigures

170 **RBI** put up by Chuck Klein in 1930. It was the second season of a historic run by the outfielder, which saw him post five consecutive campaigns with more than 120 RBI.

2 **STRIKEOUTS** recorded by Ken Raffensberger in the 1944 All-Star Game. With two shutout innings, Raffensberger became the first Phillies hurler to win the Midsummer Classic.

58 **HOMERS** belted by first baseman Ryan Howard in 2006, a franchise record. Howard won the MVP Award in his second full season in the Major Leagues.

201 **HITS** recorded by Richie Allen in 1964 during his Rookie of the Year campaign. He also hit .318 with 29 homers, 38 doubles and 13 triples.

41,626 **FANS** in attendance on April 12, 2004, when the Phillies opened Citizens Bank Park for its first game. Philadelphia fell to the Reds that day, 4-1.

0 **HITS** allowed by Philadelphia's Charles Ferguson on Aug. 29, 1885, in the first no-hitter in franchise history. Ferguson finished with a 26-20 record that year.

PITTSBURGH PIRATES

DESPITE BEING ONE OF BASEBALL'S smallest-market teams since its inception in 1882, Pittsburgh has found ways to compete. During the early 20th century, the Pirates were carried to four pennants on the broad shoulders of Honus Wagner. Much more than a name on a famous baseball card, Wagner is among a handful of legitimate contenders for the title of greatest player in MLB history. A brilliant defensive shortstop, the genial Wagner also led the league in batting average eight times, slugging six times and steals five times. At least one statistical method rated his 1908 season the best of all time, prompting baseball historian and statistician Bill James to declare that "there is no one who has ever played the game that I would be more anxious to have on a baseball team."

After a stellar run in the 1920s, the Pirates franchise entered a deep slumber for nearly 30 years. That ended in 1955, when Pittsburgh GM Branch Rickey plucked a raw outfielder named Roberto Clemente from Brooklyn's farm system. The Pirates were 108 games over .500 during the Clemente era, capturing titles in 1960 and '71. Later that decade, the "We Are Family" Pirates, featuring many players Clemente had mentored, won a title in 1979.

In the early 1990s, the emergence of Barry Bonds sparked a mini-revival with three straight NL East crowns. Pittsburgh came within one out of reaching the World Series in 1992, but Francisco Cabrera's clutch walk-off single in the NLCS won it for Atlanta and ended the Bonds era in heartbreak for Pirates fans. Almost a decade later, Pittsburgh opened what is arguably baseball's finest ballpark in 2001, and the arrival of Andrew McCutchen in 2009 gave the Pirates a franchise player to build their next winning team around.

The Pirates enjoyed unprecedented success during the years when right field was occupied by Clemente, who hit .317 for his career. He and the team capitalized on that good fortune by taking home two World Series championships — in 1960 and '71.

175

MOST CASUAL FANS WERE OBLIVIOUS TO CLEMENTE'S GREATNESS UNTIL 1971, WHEN HE BECAME A STAR DURING THE FIRST WORLD SERIES BROADCAST ON PRIMETIME TV.

TRUE GREATNESS

While most people were preparing to ring in the New Year in style on Dec. 31, 1972, a small group led by Pirates outfielder Roberto Clemente loaded a plane with supplies bound for the suffering masses in earthquake-ravaged Nicaragua. Clemente boarded that plane hoping that his presence would ensure relief actually reached the people. But minutes after taking off, the plane crashed into the waters off the coast of Clemente's native Puerto Rico, robbing baseball of one of its best and most noble men.

To "play like Roberto Clemente" would become a compliment in its own right, as Clemente had become one of the most talented hitters in the National League. He batted .314 in Pittsburgh's championship season of 1960, but it wasn't until '61 that he started playing like the true *Roberto Clemente*: a .351 average for his first batting title, 23 home runs, 201 hits and 100 runs scored. Clemente added two more batting crowns in 1964 and '65 but, ironically, it was in 1966 — when he didn't win the batting title — that Clemente was voted NL MVP.

Because Clemente spent his entire career in Pittsburgh, most casual fans were oblivious to his greatness until 1971, when he became a nationwide star during the first World Series broadcast on primetime television. While dazzling

everyone with his rocket arm, Clemente batted .414 and collected at least one hit in each game. In Game 7, his solo homer proved the difference in a 2-1 win, as Pittsburgh claimed the title. Fall Classic opponent Brooks Robinson said of Clemente, "I knew he was good, but I didn't know he was *this* good." Clemente would perish just over a year later — after collecting his 3,000th hit in his final regular season game — but his performance throughout his 18-year career ensured that baseball would never forget him.

MAZ'S BLAST

Thanks to a flourishing Bill Mazeroski and an improved pitching staff headed by Roy Face and Vern Law, Pittsburgh finished second in the National League in 1958. Combined with a late charge in '59, hope was slowly being forged at Forbes Field. Then came 1960.

The New York Yankees entered that year's World Series having won 15 straight regular-season games. Oddsmakers installed them as 5-to-7 favorites, but the Pirates managed to push the Series to a Game 7.

It was a bright summer-like afternoon in Pittsburgh on Thursday, Oct. 13. Most of the 36,683 in attendance

Although Clemente tragically died while setting out on a humanitarian mission just a few months after the 1972 season ended, his legacy as one of the greatest hitters ever endures.

Mazeroski was an unlikely hero for Pittsburgh during the 1960 World Series. His Game 7 walk-off home run brought the crown back to the Steel City for the first time in 35 years.

at Forbes Field for Game 7 had found their seats before Law fired the first pitch at 1 p.m. The teams went back and forth and back again, exchanging blows in a high-scoring affair, with the game tied at nine in the 10th.

"The first pitch I threw was high," Yankees pitcher Ralph Terry recalled decades later about the fateful at-bat with Pirates light-hitting infielder Mazeroski. "So Johnny Blanchard calls timeout and comes to the mound. He says, 'You've got to get the ball down.'"

Terry's second pitch to Mazeroski was lower, but not nearly low enough.

"I didn't know for sure if it was gone, but I knew he was not going to catch it," Mazeroski later said of left

fielder Yogi Berra. "If he misplayed it, I wanted to end up on third."

"I didn't think the ball was going to go out," Berra recalled thinking as he turned his back on the infield. "It may have even grazed the ivy."

But the ball never caromed back for Berra. It sailed over the wall, a shot that would be stamped on the memories of a generation of Pirates fans.

"I just figured it's another home run to win a ball-game," Mazeroski demurred in 2010. "But here we are 50 years later talking about it, and it's still a big thing in Pittsburgh. I hear the story of where everybody was. It was a magical moment in Pittsburgh."

A RIVER RUNS THROUGH IT

After decades of playing in the cavernous settings of Forbes Field and Three Rivers Stadium, the Pittsburgh Pirates finally broke ground on PNC Park in 1999, and their new home opened in 2001.

The franchise built the stadium near the site of its first home, Exposition Park, along the Allegheny River. The capacity is among the smallest in the Major Leagues, but while PNC provides a more intimate experience than its much-larger predecessors, it does have a number of characteristics that are similar to its forebears, such as a series of archways along the entry-level facade and decorative terra cotta elements.

Still, PNC Park has several signature elements of its own. Most notably the park provides an outstanding view of the downtown Pittsburgh skyline. In addition, the Pirates paid homage to their long and storied history by featuring statues of several of the team's greatest all-time players. They also built the right-field wall to stand 21 feet tall in honor of Hall of Fame right fielder Roberto Clemente, who wore uniform No. 21, and whose legacy in Pittsburgh — and in baseball — will always live on.

Pittsburgh's PNC Park, with its view of the Allegheny River, opened in 2001 near the site of the franchise's first stadium.

CLEMENTE, KINER, STARGELL, WAGNER — OF THE PLAYERS IN THE HALL WHO PRIMARILY PLAYED FOR THE PIRATES, ALL EARNED PAYCHECKS WITH THEIR BATWORK.

BIG HITTERS

It isn't just the World Series titles that have helped weave such a vibrant mosaic of baseball history in Pittsburgh. More important are the names that have called the city home. Roberto Clemente, Ralph Kiner, Willie Stargell, Honus Wagner — those are names found on Hall of Fame plaques, ones that stir memories of batting titles and majestic home runs. Of the players in the Hall who primarily played for the Pirates during their careers, all earned their paychecks with their batwork.

That mantle now falls to Andrew McCutchen, a young center fielder with speed and power. Like Clemente, "Cutch" has become known for his flash and grace in the field. But for all of McCutchen's accomplishments at a young age, he has a lot to live up to.

Stargell spent his entire career with the Pirates. During his 21 years in Pittsburgh, he racked up home runs and RBI, establishing franchise records with 475 and 1,540,

respectively. Nicknamed "Pops" in the latter stages of his career, Stargell was the unquestioned leader of the 1979 "We Are Family" championship club.

Wagner could still be considered the greatest player ever to don a Buccos uniform. He retired with 3,415 hits and 1,736 runs scored, both records at the time of his departure from the game.

Kiner wasn't lucky enough to enjoy the championship success that some of his Pittsburgh colleagues did, but his individual accomplishments are more than worthy of praise. A tremendous fan favorite, Kiner led the National League in home runs in each of his seven Pirates seasons. It's said that the majority of crowds would leave Forbes Field following Kiner's last at-bat of a game; he served as the main attraction of the day.

Those and others dot the halls of Cooperstown with Pirates pride, representing the Steel City's rich baseball history well with accomplishments that continue to withstand the test of time.

Clockwise from top left: Wagner, Stargell, Kiner and 1978 NL MVP Dave Parker drew fans to Pittsburgh with their prowess at the plate.

Pirates Hall of Famers

MAX CAREY . . . . . . Played excellent defense and stole 738 bases.

FRED CLARKE . . . . . Future skipper went 5 for 5 in his first game.

ROBERTO CLEMENTE . Recorded 3,000 hits and possessed one of the strongest and most accurate arms in baseball history.

RALPH KINER . . . . . Averaged more than 100 RBI and more than 36 homers a year during his 10-year career.

BILL MAZEROSKI . . . . Won eight Gold Glove Awards at second base.

WILLIE STARGELL . . . Took home the 1979 NL MVP Award and belted 475 homers while knocking in 1,540 runs.

PIE TRAYNOR . . . . . . Hit .320 over 17 seasons and never struck out more than 28 times.

ARKY VAUGHAN . . . . Raked at a .385 clip in 1935 to lead the NL.

HONUS WAGNER . . . Recorded a .327 career average with 3,415 hits.

LLOYD WANER . . . . . The younger Waner had 223 hits as a rookie.

PAUL WANER . . . . . . Had a .333 career average over 20 seasons.

ST. LOUIS CARDINALS

ARGUABLY THE MOST SUCCESSFUL franchise in National League history, the St. Louis Cardinals have won 11 World Series — more than any other team but the Yankees. Their first title was perhaps the most memorable. In 1926 the Cards picked up 39-year-old legend Grover Cleveland "Pete" Alexander off waivers, and he proved pivotal to their world championship by going 2-0 with a 1.33 ERA and 17 strikeouts in 20.1 Fall Classic innings, including 2.1 frames of no-hit relief work to secure a 3-2 win in the tightly fought Game 7.

Around the same time, visionary executive Branch Rickey was making waves in the front office. Rickey invented what is today known as the farm system, churning out future Hall of Famers Dizzy Dean, Joe Medwick, Johnny Mize and Stan Musial, among many others. Dean and Medwick were the ringleaders of the boisterous "Gashouse Gang" that won the 1934 World Series, while Musial, called up in 1941, led St. Louis to the pennant in each of his first four full seasons. By the time "Stan the Man" retired in 1963, he was the NL's all-time leader in hits, doubles, runs and RBI.

Musial also mentored the next generation of Cardinals players who won the World Series one year after his retirement, including Bob Gibson, Ken Boyer and Curt Flood. Another championship followed in 1967, with Gibson hurling three complete-game wins in the Fall Classic. A few years later, Manager Whitey Herzog constructed a stellar speed-and-defense team that won pennants in 1982, '85 and '87. Another glory era began in 2001, when rookie Albert Pujols turned in the first of 10 straight seasons with at least a .300 average, 30 home runs and 100 RBI. During the 11 years that Pujols anchored the lineup, the Cards made the playoffs seven times and won the World Series twice, including in his final year with the team.

GIBSON'S 1968 SEASON RANKS AS THE BEST BY A PITCHER IN MODERN BASE-BALL HISTORY. NOT ONLY DID HE WIN THE NL CY YOUNG AWARD, BUT HE ALSO WAS NAMED THE LEAGUE'S MVP.

Gibson's 1968 season ranks as the best by a pitcher in modern baseball history. He compiled a miniscule 1.12 ERA, a modern record, to go with 22 wins and NL-leading totals of 13 shutouts and 268 strikeouts. Not only did Gibson win the NL Cy Young Award, but he also was named the league's MVP.

Gibson was the winning pitcher in Game 7 in both the 1964 and 1967 World Series and set a Fall Classic record with 17 strikeouts in Game 1 of the 1968 edition.

Gibson continued to excel into the 1970s. He won his second Cy Young Award in 1970 and tossed a no-hitter against the Pittsburgh Pirates on Aug. 14, 1971. Three seasons later, on July 17, 1974, he became just the second Big League pitcher ever to reach 3,000 career strikeouts (following the Washington Senators' Walter Johnson). Gibson was inducted into the Hall of Fame in 1981.

ARMED AND DANGEROUS

A first-ballot Hall of Fame inductee, Gibson's fearsome reputation caused opposing batters to cower, tilting the advantage even further toward the pitcher's side. The Cardinals' pitching record book is essentially a Gibson biography.

The late 1960s and 1970s were largely dominated by pitching, and epitomized by right-hander Bob Gibson. A standout basketball player at Creighton University in his hometown of Omaha, Neb., Gibson was signed by Cardinals scout Runt Marr in 1957 and went on to pitch in the Majors from 1959–75 — all with St. Louis. He possessed a blazing fastball, pinpoint control and a fiercely competitive temperament. Among the categories for which Gibson sits atop the Cardinals' record book are wins (251), complete games (255), shutouts (56) and strikeouts (3,117). An elite athlete, he also hit 24 career homers and won nine Gold Glove Awards.

SURGING TO THE TOP

The Cardinals did their part on the last day of the 2011 season. They had just beaten the Astros in Game 162 to ensure that they would at least have a play-in game to wrest

Freese tied Game 6 of the 2011 Fall Classic with two outs in the bottom of the ninth, so when it came time to end things in the 11th, it was, of course, Freese who delivered the walk-off home run to force a Game 7.

the NL Wild Card from the Braves, who had, a little over a month earlier, held a 10.5-game lead. But a one-game play-off became moot when the Braves lost to the Phillies later that night, giving St. Louis a shocking playoff berth.

Albert Pujols had seen his crew shake off a rough August to somehow claw back into a race in which it had no business being a part. It was an amazing march, the kind that people talk about forever. And yet, that night of Game 162 would be just the beginning. The Phillies were unbeatable, but the Cardinals beat them in five games in the NLDS. The Brewers' lineup was unstoppable, until St. Louis's pitchers stopped them in six contests.

And yet the amazing thing about the decisive moment of a great Fall Classic wasn't how quickly it all happened. It was that it felt like it took forever.

Rangers closer Neftali Feliz started his delivery in Game 6 of the World Series with a 7-5 lead and a chance to bring a title to Texas, but the pitch met David Freese's bat. Nine seconds later, two runs had scored, and Freese slid into third, tying the game and saving the Cardinals' season.

"I thought I got a good piece of it," Freese later recalled. "I saw Nelson Cruz break back, and then, rounding first base, I thought he was going to catch it. Fortunately, it fell."

Two innings later, when Freese homered, the Cards had forced a Game 7, a cinch in comparison to the rest of their ascent. The Cards became champs for the 11th time the next night, winners of the best Fall Classic in a decade. They are going to talk about Freese there forever, as well as Tony La Russa and Allen Craig and Chris Carpenter. They'll be talking about a game that lasted four hours and 33 minutes, but really, they'll be talking about three seconds, from the moment Freese connected against Feliz to the point when the ball sailed past Cruz's glove.

The 2011 St. Louis Cardinals will be remembered for finishing the story, for fighting back. They will be remembered for the fact that they handled adversity and never gave up. And they'll be remembered for a handful of seconds on a cold Thursday night in October, when a ball held up just long enough for a flock of Cardinals to lift a city on its wings.

The Cardinals still had plenty of work left to do after Freese's walk-off job in Game 6 of the 2011 World Series, but realistically speaking, the Fall Classic was already over. After weeks of drama, the team wasn't about to sink in its final test.

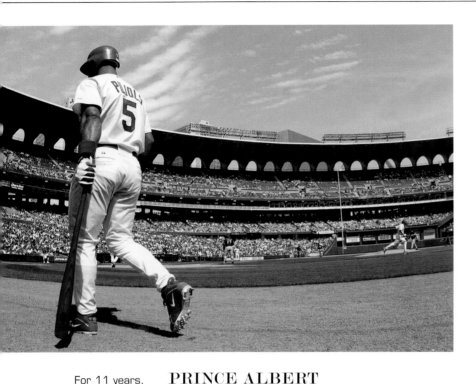

vendors made sure to walk down a staircase so as not to disrespect the moment by turning their backs. Ushers left their posts. The rest of the St. Louis Cardinals turned into an admiration society at the sheer hypnosis of the moment: Pujols waggling his bat, his fans turning to putty at the possibility of what might happen.

A near–home run was seen as the best-case scenario. The level of reverence for Albert Pujols, baseball player, during his 11 years with the Cardinals was unmatched among his peers and unseen in the game for generations. His consistency was obvious.

It's not just that Pujols may have had the best 10-year stretch ever to start a career, that he hit more homers and doubles over that span than anyone in the NL. It's that every single year he puts up mind-boggling numbers. He rarely has an off-day, let alone an off-week, month or, laughably, year. Even 2011, despite a slow start, saw him finish hitting .311 from May through season's end.

"I honestly believe he's the best hitter in the history of the game," said his former teammate in St. Louis, Lance Berkman. "Not just today. Ever."

Although he departed St. Louis for Anaheim after the 2011 season, Pujols' achievements will not soon be forgotten by the loyal denizens of Busch Stadium. And from the plate to the mound to the stands and beyond, fans all watch and appreciate, hypnotized by possibility. After all these years, Pujols still has the entire sport entranced. We're not rushing to snap our fingers, either.

For 11 years, Pujols defined the Cardinals, leading them to two world championships and becoming one of the club's all-time greats. Saying goodbye after 2011 was hard, but there were plenty of memories left behind.

PRINCE ALBERT

Every time Albert Pujols stepped into the batter's box for the St. Louis Cardinals, he held rapt an entire ballpark. Fans peered from luxury boxes and upper-deck seats located in another zip code hoping to witness greatness. Beer

Cardinals Hall of Famers

JIM BOTTOMLEY . . . . Hit .300 nine times in 16 years.
LOU BROCK . . . . Accumulated 3,023 hits.
DIZZY DEAN . . . . Led the league in K's four straight times.
FRANKIE FRISCH . . . . Won the MVP Award in 1931.
BOB GIBSON . . . . Won 251 games and an MVP and two Cy Young awards.
CHICK HAFEY . . . . Hit .317 with a .372 OBP for his career.
JESSE HAINES . . . . Went 2-0 in the 1926 World Series.
ROGERS HORNSBY . . . . Topped the .400 mark three times.
JOHNNY MIZE . . . . Recorded six three-homer games in his career.
JOE MEDWICK . . . . Won the 1937 MVP Award.
STAN MUSIAL . . . . Knocked 3,630 hits and won three MVP Awards.
RED SCHOENDIENST . . . . A superb second baseman who got 10 All-Star nods.
ENOS SLAUGHTER . . . . Won the 1946 Series with his "mad dash."
OZZIE SMITH . . . . Made 15 All-Star teams while playing a stellar shortstop.
BRUCE SUTTER . . . . Led the NL in saves five times.

THE MAN

Stan Musial played his entire 22-year career, from 1941–63, in St. Louis, and is widely considered the greatest player in Cardinals history. Once a pitcher in the Cards' farm system, Musial owned or shared 29 National League records, 17 Big League marks and stood alone atop the Cardinals' leaderboard in numerous statistical categories upon retiring in 1963. Musial's 24 appearances in the Midsummer Classic tie him with fellow Hall of Famers Hank Aaron and Willie Mays for the most in a career. He holds All-Star Game records for most home runs (six) and most pinch-hits (three), and is tied with Mays for most extra-base hits (eight) and total bases (40). Musial led the NL in batting seven times and won three MVP Awards — in 1943, '46 and '48. He has the fourth-most hits in baseball history, trailing just Pete Rose, Ty Cobb and Hank Aaron.

The pride of Donora, Pa., and adopted son of the city of St. Louis would become the Cardinals' GM in 1967 and preside over the club's World Series crown that year, the fourth championship he helped bring the franchise.

"All Musial represents," said St. Louis resident and acclaimed broadcaster Bob Costas, "is more than two decades of sustained excellence and complete decency as a human being."

Musial was the first Redbird to have his uniform number retired, and as a lifelong Cardinal, he's revered in St. Louis, where a statue depicting his famed batting stance greets fans at Busch Stadium's third-base entry. "Stan Musial is as much a St. Louis monument as the Gateway Arch," author Peter Golenbock wrote in *The Spirit of St. Louis*, published in 2000. "He was a fixture who could be counted on to be a hometown hero to children and adults alike."

Musial's succinct nickname — "The Man" — is among the most to-the-point in all of sports. And it perfectly reflects how all fans — not just those wearing red — feel about the legendary hitter and franchise cornerstone.

Cardinals history is really a story of sustained excellence, from the franchise's founding in 1882 through the World Series championship in 2011. But few teams have inspired more anecdotes than the Gashouse Gang of the 1930s (above). Two of the most famed members of the 1934 team, brothers Dizzy and Daffy Dean, paired their off-field shenanigans with dominance between the lines.

IN '34, DIZZY DEAN PUT TOGETHER THE BEST SEASON OF HIS CAREER, AND BECAME THE FIRST OF THREE REDBIRDS PITCHERS TO WIN THE NATIONAL LEAGUE MVP AWARD.

WINNING TRADITION

Widely regarded as the game's greatest right-handed hitter, Rogers Hornsby won seven batting titles — topping the magical .400 mark an astounding three times — including 1924, when his .424 average set a mark that still stands as a modern-era NL record.

Between 1900 and 1925, though, the Cardinals finished as high as third place in the NL just four times. On May 31, 1925, Hornsby replaced Branch Rickey as the Cardinals' manager (still retaining his playing duties) while Rickey remained with the team in the front office. Hornsby served in the dual role in 1926, piloting the club to an 89-65 record and its first world championship, a seven-game victory over Babe Ruth's Yankees. Another title, this one also going seven games, came in 1931.

The 1934 Cardinals, dubbed the "Gashouse Gang", boasted a swashbuckling collection of players led by three born-and-bred Redbirds: pitcher Dizzy Dean, outfielder/third baseman Pepper Martin and outfielder Joe Medwick. Dean and Medwick have plaques in the Hall of Fame, while Martin was selected to four All-Star teams. The Gang led the club to its third world title that year.

Dean put together the best season of his career in '34, going 30-7 with a 2.66 ERA and 195 strikeouts, and became the first of three Redbirds pitchers to win the NL MVP Award.

A whirling dervish on the basepaths, the 5-foot-8 Martin led the league in stolen bases in 1933, '34 and '36. "The Wild Horse of the Osage" played in two Fall Classics with St. Louis, and his .418 average (23 for 55) ranks as the third highest among players with at least 40 plate appearances.

Not to be outdone, Medwick is the last NL player to win the Triple Crown, doing so in 1937 with a .374 average, 31 homers and 154 RBI — a franchise record — that earned him MVP honors. Medwick never once hit below .300 in seven full campaigns with the Cardinals en route to being inducted into the Hall of Fame.

Birds of a Feather

.401 **BATTING AVERAGE** posted by Rogers Hornsby in 1922, the year he won the Triple Crown in the National League. Hornsby also hit 42 homers with 152 RBI.

.353 **BATTING AVERAGE** recorded by Willie McGee in 1985, then an NL record for a switch-hitter. McGee won the MVP Award that year, also leading the NL with 216 hits.

5 **HOME RUNS** belted by Hall of Famer Stan Musial during one doubleheader on May 2, 1954, against the New York Giants at Busch Stadium in St. Louis.

3 **HITS** allowed by Dizzy Dean in his first career start. On Sept. 28, 1930, with the pennant race already decided in St. Louis's favor, the 20-year-old earned a complete-game win.

2 **GRAND SLAMS** hit by Fernando Tatis in the same inning on April 23, 1999, both off of the Dodgers' Chan Ho Park. That year, Tatis tied a then-club record with three slams.

106 **WINS** posted by the 1942 Cardinals, a club record. Led by Musial, Enos Slaughter and Mort Cooper, the Redbirds went on to win the World Series in five games over the Yankees.

SAN DIEGO PADRES

W ITH A LEGACY THAT includes a tie to the last man to bat .400 and the last man to challenge the mark — Ted Williams and Tony Gwynn, respectively — San Diego has a rich baseball heritage. Williams got his start with the Minor League version of the Padres in 1936, and by 1969 there were enough rabid baseball fans in San Diego for MLB to place an expansion team there. The new Padres made a splash in 1973 by drafting star college pitcher Dave Winfield, converting him to the outfield and bringing him straight to the Majors, where he eventually became the first Hall of Famer to wear a Padres cap on his plaque.

The Padres have posted a .463 winning percentage over their history, worse than any Big League team except the Rays. But the bright moments and colorful characters have been plentiful as well. Over the years, San Diegans have fallen in love with Vaseline-toting hurler Gaylord Perry, shortstop wizard Ozzie Smith, classy closer Trevor Hoffman and San Diego native Adrian Gonzalez, among many others. In 1984 the Friars captured their first NL pennant thanks in large part to Steve Garvey's clutch ninth-inning homer in Game 4 of the NLCS. The main star of that team, though, was Gwynn, a lithe, speedy hitting machine who won the first of his eight batting titles with a .351 mark. Fourteen years later, in 1998, the Padres won a second pennant, with a slightly thicker version of Gwynn still leading the team in hitting. Other clubs may have won more throughout their history than the Padres, but precious few have a franchise player as universally beloved as Gwynn.

The former record holder for career saves, Hoffman helped lead San Diego to the World Series in 1998.

He knew that in order to get the Padres back atop the National League West, where they finished in his first season as GM in 1996, many more changes would have to occur, particularly in the bullpen.

So he continued going about the business of changing the face of the Padres club for '98, and in the end, the Padres' amazing turnaround season speaks for itself. By Sept. 12, they had clinched their second NL West championship in three years, their third overall.

Greg Vaughn, Trevor Hoffman and Brown were just three of the team's five All-Stars. The Padres also got outstanding contributions from holdover stars Wally Joyner, Quilvio Veras, Steve Finley and Ken Caminiti. But what many believe pushed the Padres over the top that season was the so-called supporting cast.

Towers kept tinkering with the bullpen well into the season, acquiring Randy Myers from Toronto in August, giving the club a legitimate left-handed threat out of the bullpen in the late innings, something Towers had been seeking for years.

When his tweaking and adjusting was complete, Towers saw his many parts come together to form a whole in October. Stellar pitching limited the Astros to eight runs in four games in the Division Series, and four of the six NLCS games saw the Atlanta Braves limited to two or fewer runs.

Their momentum ran out in the World Series against the Yankees, but the mix-and-match Padres' run to the pennant remains a memorable one.

MIX 'N' MATCH

When Kevin Towers engineered the biggest trade of his tenure as the Padres' general manager before the 1998 season, he might have just put his feet up and relaxed. After all, he had just acquired ace Kevin Brown, generally considered among the top three or four starting pitchers in the game at the time.

Instead, Towers rolled up his sleeves and just kept working — acquiring was only part of what Towers wanted to accomplish in the wake of a disappointing '97 season.

LEADING MAN

As a young athlete, Hall of Famer Tony Gwynn was world class. Recruited by San Diego State's basketball team as a speedy point guard, Gwynn's dual-threat abilities were on display during the weekend of March 7–9, 1981, when he had a 16-point, 16-assist game in basketball, followed two days later by a baseball doubleheader in which he drove in the winning run in both games. Three months later, the Padres and the NBA's Clippers drafted him on the same day.

He picked baseball, and in 1984, Gwynn won his first batting title while leading San Diego to its first pennant. By 1987, he had become a spectacular all-around player, batting a league-best .370 while also stealing 56 bases and winning the second of his five Gold Gloves. From 1993–97 he hit at least .350 every year, winning four of his NL-record eight batting titles. Over his final nine seasons,

"MY FATHER SAID IF YOU WORK HARD, GOOD THINGS WILL HAPPEN. BOY, OH BOY, HE WAS ABSOLUTELY RIGHT." — *TONY GWYNN*

Gwynn was most known for his sweet swing and eight batting titles, but his athleticism was underrated. For much of his career, he could also steal his share of bases.

Gwynn never hit below .321. His status as one of the best hitters ever rested largely on hard work and preparation; perhaps no batter in baseball history studied the art of hitting as intensely as Gwynn, or prepared so assiduously. It was Gwynn who popularized the use of video to study and perfect his mechanics, and nobody was ever better at slapping line-drive singles to the opposite field.

Gwynn's finest moment came in 1994, when he snuck achingly close to the .400 mark. His average hovered in the .380s for most of the year, but in early August it surged. When a players' strike prematurely ended the season on Aug. 12, Gwynn's average stood at .394, the highest since Ted Williams' .406 53 years earlier. Gwynn's contact skills were so advanced, he struck out fewer than 20 times in eight different seasons in which he had at least 400 plate appearances, including the strike-shortened '94 and '95 seasons. The only modern-era player to do that more often was Nellie Fox, who never struck out more than 18 times in any season.

"My father said if you work hard, good things will happen," Gwynn said in his Hall of Fame induction speech. "Boy, oh boy, he was absolutely right."

Winfield exploded onto the Big League scene without having played one day in the Minor Leagues.

WINFIELD, MANY WOULD ARGUE, IS ONE OF THE HALF-DOZEN BEST ATHLETES EVER TO SET FOOT ON A MAJOR LEAGUE DIAMOND.

SUPERMAN

Dave Winfield's Big League career — one filled with agents, publicists and an entertainer's lifestyle — was a preview of the modern-day athlete. Winfield embraced the free-agency era and, playing with six teams over a 21-year Major League career, embodied it better than any other player of his generation.

Winfield, many would argue, is one of the half-dozen best athletes ever to set foot on a Major League diamond. Consider that at the University of Minnesota in 1973, he batted .385 while going 9-1 as a pitcher and winning the Most Outstanding Player Award of the College World Series. He also remains the only player drafted in three different sports: baseball, basketball and football, a sport he had never even played at any organized level before. After signing with the Padres, he skipped the Minor Leagues, bringing his impressive tools directly to the Majors. During eight seasons with the Padres, he transformed himself from a raw talent into one of the best all-around players in the game — but few outside of San Diego took note of the expansion Padres' talented outfielder.

Winfield finally became a national figure in 1981, when he signed a 10-year, $20 million-plus free agent contract with the New York Yankees, making him the highest-paid player in baseball history to that point. Despite all the pressures of a big contract, he was still the Yankees' most productive hitter of the decade, walloping 203 home runs with New York and topping 100 RBI six times in seven years as a player in the Bronx.

After leaving the Yankees in 1989, Winfield drifted through the AL, serving brief stints with four teams. His lone year as a Toronto Blue Jay in 1992 gave Winfield his only World Series title, and his two seasons with the Twins enabled the St. Paul native to collect his 3,000th hit in front of his hometown fans. He retired in 1995 with a legacy that includes 465 homers and 3,110 hits. Back when 20 home runs was a significant feat, Winfield reached that number in 18 straight years before the 1994 strike broke his streak.

SD *Father Figures*

50 BASES or more stolen by three different Padres players in 1980, becoming the first team in history to accomplish that feat in a single season. Gene Richards (61) led the way, followed by Ozzie Smith (57) and Jerry Mumphrey (52).

22 WINS posted by Randy Jones in 1976 to nab the club's first Cy Young Award. He also recorded league-bests in WHIP (1.027), complete games (25) and innings pitched (315.1).

98 VICTORIES, a franchise record set by the 1998 Padres. That total was good enough for first place in the National League West by 9.5 games over the San Francisco Giants.

.351 BATTING AVERAGE posted by Tony Gwynn in 1984 to win the first of his eight batting titles. Gwynn, who hit .338 in his career, would finish with eight batting crowns.

479 CAREER SAVES recorded by righty Trevor Hoffman to become baseball's all-time leader on Sept. 24, 2006, against the Pirates. The next season he became the first pitcher to surpass 500 saves, but both marks were bested by Mariano Rivera in 2011.

1,027 CONSECUTIVE GAMES played by first baseman Steve Garvey before a dislocated thumb ended his streak in July 1983. The run set a National League record.

SAN FRANCISCO GIANTS

NO FRANCHISE IN MLB HISTORY has won more total games than the Giants, who have amassed more than 10,500 victories in more than 125 years of existence splitting time between New York and San Francisco. They've won at a stunning .538 clip, a mark better than every other Big League team but the Yankees.

It was in 1902, when skipper John McGraw and pitcher Christy Mathewson first paired up, that the Giants started to become one of the Majors' most dominant forces and most prestigious franchises. The profane McGraw and the reverent Mathewson seemed an odd couple, but they combined for five pennants and one championship from 1904–13. By 1925, McGraw was nearing retirement, but he was still baseball's savviest talent finder, signing 16-year-old Mel Ott and tutoring him until he became one of the greatest hitters in baseball history.

The Giants scored another scouting coup in 1950 when they discovered a skinny 19-year-old named Willie Mays playing in the dying Negro Leagues. The rookie was on deck when Bobby Thomson hit the franchise's most famous homer in 1951, and remained the rock of the lineup after the franchise moved west. With Mays joined by Juan Marichal, Willie McCovey and Orlando Cepeda, the Giants captured the 1962 pennant in an epic battle with the Dodgers. They then came within inches of winning Game 7 of the World Series when McCovey hit a scorching line drive with two men in scoring position that happened to find the mitt of the Yankees' perfectly placed second baseman — Bobby Richardson — for the final out. Forty years later, this time behind the historic bat of Mays' godson, Barry Bonds, the Giants appeared in yet another Fall Classic — only to lose Game 7 again. The face of the Giants' first title team in San Francisco turned out to be not Mays or Bonds, but Tim Lincecum, the scrawny right-hander with a stupendous fastball who helped hurl the club to the 2010 championship.

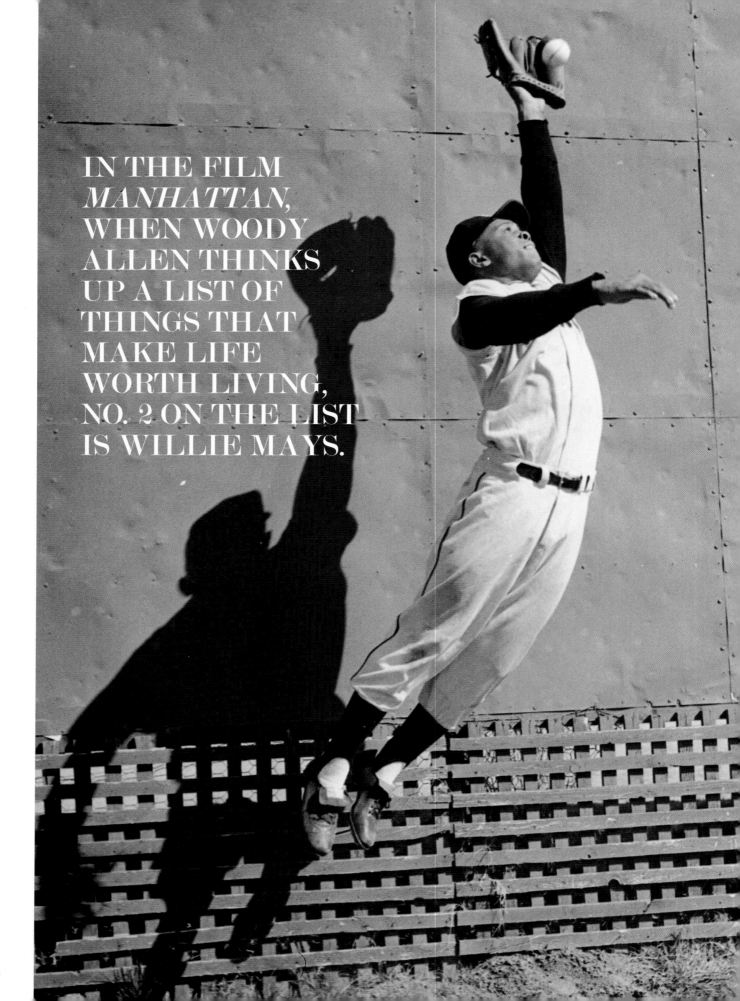

IN THE FILM *MANHATTAN*, WHEN WOODY ALLEN THINKS UP A LIST OF THINGS THAT MAKE LIFE WORTH LIVING, NO. 2 ON THE LIST IS WILLIE MAYS.

SAY HEY

With 12 Gold Gloves, 660 homers, four stolen base titles and a .302 lifetime batting average in a pitchers' era, Willie Mays brought more to the table than any other player in baseball history.

At his peak in the mid-1950s, Mays was arguably the best in baseball at each of the five essential tools: hitting for average, hitting for power, fielding, running and throwing. No player has ever come close to matching that. The most memorable example of Mays' fielding prowess is his fabled over-the-shoulder catch of a Vic Wertz shot during the 1954 World Series, a 450-foot drive that he claimed he had all the way.

Mays was no mere natural ballplayer, but one who perfected his game far away from the spotlight during a three-year apprenticeship in the Negro Leagues. The son of well-known semi-pro player William Mays Sr., Willie grew up in Birmingham, Ala., and joined the local Negro Leagues team, the Black Barons, while still in high school. There, he absorbed the wisdom of two mentors — veteran Negro Leaguers Piper Davis and Artie Wilson — and by the time he entered the Giants' farm system in 1950, he was already a complete player. During his rookie year with the Giants, Mays was known to forget his teammates' names, and often used a playful "Say Hey" greeting to address his peers. That spirited greeting eventually became Mays' calling card after New York sportswriter Barney Kremenko dubbed him the "Say Hey Kid."

Throughout the 1950s and early '60s, as he quickly grew to baseball maturity, the "Kid" was the darling of baseball fans far and wide. He won his first MVP Award in 1954, following a campaign in which he posted a .345 average, rocked 41 home runs and logged 110 RBI, and capped the season with that over-the-shoulder grab in the World Series.

After day games at the Polo Grounds, Mays was known to play stickball with youngsters on 155th Street in Harlem — not for the cameras, but because he had fun doing it. People often spoke of Mays the way they spoke of royalty — in hushed tones of awe and reverence. By the 1960s Mays had become a cultural signpost — no matter where you looked, there was Willie being discussed in Bob Dylan's songs or Woody Allen's movies or Charles Schulz's *Peanuts* cartoons. In the film *Manhattan*, when Allen's character thinks up a list of things that make life worth living, No. 2 on the list is Willie Mays. Most who saw him play would agree.

BALLPARK BY THE BAY

After 40 years of calling Candlestick Park home — and sharing it with the NFL's San Francisco 49ers — the Giants moved into a downtown ballpark in 2000. AT&T Park, as it became known in 2006, is one of the most picturesque facilities built in the modern era.

The brick facade is highlighted by two 122-foot King Street clock towers, each topped by a 45-foot flagpole. Passing a statue of Giants Hall of Famer Willie Mays at the ballpark's main entrance, fans follow an indoor walkway that circles the entire park. A stunning view from the walkway reveals the China Basin area in the Bay beyond the outfield walls, as well as the world's largest baseball glove in left-center, as the scents of garlic fries and crab cake sandwiches fill the air.

While the right-field wall is just 309 feet down the line, it's 25 feet high in that area, and there's a pedestrian concourse that a ball has to clear before it can reach the water. This sidewalk beyond the wall commemorates memorable moments in the club's storied history.

Adventurous fans can be found beyond the right-field fence, hoping for a home run to clear the wall and sail into what is popularly called McCovey Cove, named for Giants Hall of Fame first baseman Willie McCovey, a statue of whom fans can find across the Cove.

A signature feature of the Giants' AT&T Park, McCovey Cove lures fans — and their sea vessels — in hopes of a souvenir.

One of the most picturesque ballparks in all of the Major Leagues, the downtown venue that is now known as AT&T Park became the Giants' home at the dawn of the millenium.

 San Francisco Treats

3 **SHUTOUTS** thrown by Christy Mathewson in the 1905 World Series, leading the Giants to a win over Philadelphia. Mathewson also whiffed 18 in his 27 scoreless innings.

2,583 **GAMES** won by Hall of Fame Manager John McGraw as skipper of the New York Giants from 1902–32. During those years, McGraw won 10 National League pennants and three World Series.

4 **BASE HITS** in as many at-bats recorded by Willie McCovey in his Major League debut on July 30, 1959. McCovey went on to win the Rookie of the Year Award that season after posting a .656 slugging percentage.

1 **HOME RUN** hit by San Francisco's slugging first baseman Will Clark in his Major League debut on April 8, 1986. The longball came off Hall of Fame hurler Nolan Ryan.

2 **MVP AWARDS** won by pitcher Carl Hubbell. The Hall of Famer spent his entire 16-year career with the Giants, winning 253 games and making nine All-Star teams.

12 **GOLD GLOVE AWARDS** won by legendary Giants center fielder Willie Mays, beginning with the first year the award was bestowed, in 1957. Only famed Pittsburgh Pirate Roberto Clemente has taken home as many among outfielders.

In one of the most memorable at-bats ever, Thomson (with hand raised) sent a Branca pitch over the fence at the Polo Grounds for the "Shot Heard 'Round the World," clinching the Giants' 1951 World Series berth.

BATTLE OF THE BOROUGHS

The 1951 National League pennant race stretched the limits of credulity, and the Brooklyn Dodgers looked like a sure thing when they held a 13.5-game lead over the second-place New York Giants on Aug. 11. Yet the Giants managed to go 37-7 down the stretch to tie the Dodgers and force a three-game playoff series to determine who would go to the World Series.

Fittingly, the drama lasted until the final pitch of the third game. The Dodgers carried a 4-1 lead into the bottom of the ninth at the Polo Grounds. Then the game took an abrupt turn: After narrowing the deficit to 4-2, outfielder Bobby Thomson hit a three-run shot — dubbed the "Shot Heard 'Round the World" — off Ralph Branca to give New York a 5-4 victory and propel the Giants into the World Series.

Red Smith of the *New York Herald-Tribune* penned a column that captured the air of shock that swept through the dugouts, the stands and the press box.

"Now it is done," Smith wrote. "Now the story ends. And there is no way to tell it. The art of fiction is dead. Reality has strangled invention. Only the utterly impossible, the inexpressibly fantastic, can ever be plausible again."

The drama still lingered 50 years later. In 2001, *Wall Street Journal* reporter Joshua Harris Prager revealed that the Giants had installed a telescope in the outfield scoreboard to relay stolen catchers' signs to the dugout with a buzzer system. Although Thomson denied knowing what pitch was coming, Prager's report added an intriguing new slant to an event already filled with drama, giving the "Shot" a new echo for a new generation.

THE FREAK'S SHOW

The first few years of Tim Lincecum's career were truly awesome, but it's a reach to peg him for the Hall of Fame already. In fact, if their careers all ended today, not a single member of the 2010 Giants would necessarily stand out as a surefire bet to add to the club's roster in Cooperstown.

But somehow, the rag-tag bunch known as the 2010 San Francisco Giants did what Orlando Cepeda, Juan Marichal, Willie McCovey and so many more never could. Cody Ross, Juan Uribe and Madison Bumgarner accomplished it, but not Barry Bonds, Matt Williams or Gaylord Perry. The San Francisco Giants were world champions, and never before had this most eclectic of West Coast cities been able to boast of that.

The 2010 season was, in a way, a fitting microcosm of that past, full of fits and starts. With Lincecum, the club was blessed with some of the finest pitching around, yet too often it seemed that if it wasn't a shutout, it wasn't enough. But then things started clicking, and after a series of wild and improbable events, the Giants found themselves the last team standing. They had finally done it; they were finally champions.

That road began with Lincecum, the 5-foot-11 toothpick with the crazy delivery. He won Game 1 in all three of the Giants' postseason series, beating the Phillies' Roy Halladay in the NLCS and the Rangers' Cliff Lee in the World Series. Not as though that was anything really *new* for Lincecum, who earned two Cy Young Awards — in 2008 and 2009 — and four 200-strikeout seasons before turning 28. Even so, he might say his crowning achievement is an eight-inning, 10-strikeout win in Game 5 of the World Series; a worthy title-clinching performance.

"It sounds ridiculous," closer Brian Wilson said after the clinch, unable to comprehend this combination of San Francisco Giants and world champions. "And I love every minute of it."

Lifted to championship status by Lincecum and the rest of the pitching staff, the 2010 Giants returned the favor and hoisted their ace after their World Series win.

SEATTLE MARINERS

CONSIDERING THAT THE MARINERS have been around for just 35 years, they have boasted an unbelievable amount of star power. There's Randy Johnson, arguably the greatest left-handed pitcher in history; Alex Rodriguez, maybe the second-greatest shortstop; and Edgar Martinez, perhaps the greatest designated hitter. Throw in 600–home run hitter Ken Griffey Jr., and baseball's most unique player in Japanese import Ichiro Suzuki, and you've got a franchise with more legendary names than some clubs that have been around for a century.

Of course, the reason the Mariners were able to draft both Griffey and Rodriguez No. 1 overall is because the team struggled for a long time. It took the Mariners until their 15th season to post their first winning record, and until their 18th to finish better than fourth place. But in 1995, they emerged as contenders in one of baseball history's greatest pennant races, which ended with Johnson pitching a three-hitter in a one-game playoff to clinch the AL West. Six days later, the most important moment in franchise history up to that point came when Martinez's double down the line drove in Griffey with the ALDS-winning run.

Johnson was traded away in 1998, Griffey in 2000, and Rodriguez left via free agency before the 2001 season — but despite the loss of three superstars, the team stunned baseball in 2001 to power its way to an astonishing, Major League–record-tying 116 victories. More recently, Felix Hernandez has established himself among the best pitchers in the game, and young stars like Jesus Montero and Justin Smoak represent the new era of budding M's stars.

Ichiro came to America in 2001 and immediately became a main draw all over the Majors. Fans chose him as an All-Star in each of his first 10 seasons.

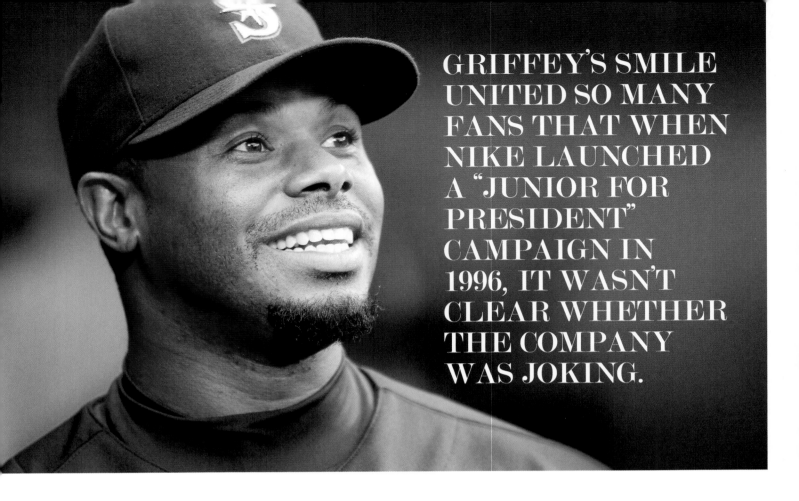

GRIFFEY'S SMILE UNITED SO MANY FANS THAT WHEN NIKE LAUNCHED A "JUNIOR FOR PRESIDENT" CAMPAIGN IN 1996, IT WASN'T CLEAR WHETHER THE COMPANY WAS JOKING.

THE KID

Ken Griffey Jr. was supposed to spend the 1989 campaign in the Minors. The Mariners believed that their 1987 top draft pick needed another year of seasoning before following in the steps of his dad, an outfielder and member of the "Big Red Machine."

The decision was such a foregone conclusion that just one of the five major baseball card manufacturers included Griffey in its 1989 set. But when the 19-year-old batted .359 and set team Spring Training records with 33 hits and 21 RBI, both the Mariners and Upper Deck officials realized that they had a Big League product on their hands — and he wouldn't disappoint.

While other sluggers may have enjoyed higher home run totals or longer careers than Griffey, few players have been so beloved. From the day he first arrived in the Major Leagues wearing a backwards cap and a diamond earring, fans took to him as if they had known him their entire lives. They marveled at the beauty of his left-handed stroke, reveled in his acrobatic circus catches in center field and celebrated in 1990 when he and his father hit back-to-back home runs for the Mariners. "Grif was happy-go-lucky every day," recalled Bronson Arroyo, who followed Griffey's career as a youngster before becoming his teammate in Cincinnati. "Everybody enjoyed him being around all the time. I just imagined him being the same as he was as a young kid."

"Junior" grew up in Big League clubhouses and treated his rookie season like any other day at the ballpark. With his youthful energy and ever-present smile, it was no wonder teammates called him "The Kid." At 6 feet, 3 inches and 195 pounds, the Seattle center fielder played with a skill and elegance few of his contemporaries could match, winning a Most Valuable Player Award in 1997. The elder Griffey liked to say that as a hitter, Junior most resembled Hall of Fame Cardinals legend Stan Musial. "It's a great compliment to be compared to Kenny," Musial responded.

Part of Griffey's appeal was that his excellence seemed effortless. Of course, one doesn't hit 630 Major League homers or drive in 140-plus runs three straight seasons without expending massive amounts of blood, sweat and tears. Nor does one post seven 40-homer seasons or win 10 Gold Gloves without working at it a little. But Griffey always seemed to enjoy himself so much that it hardly seemed like work. He never shied away from expressing joy, especially during sublime moments like the 1995 ALDS, when he exuberantly slid home with the series-winning run against the Yankees. Everybody rooted for Junior. His smile united so many fans that when Nike launched a "Junior For President" campaign in 1996, it wasn't clear whether the company was joking.

The "Junior for Hall" campaign won't need much help. When he becomes eligible after the 2015 season, his passage into Cooperstown is all but a sure thing.

Griffey's Major League pedigree was reason enough to believe he would be special, but no one could have predicted a career that would see him crush 630 homers and make 13 All-Star teams.

Reynolds, who became a TV analyst after his playing career, was a headliner back in the days when the Mariners weren't producing too many All-Stars.

FAN FAVORITE

Harold Reynolds was the club's first two-time All-Star and first premier defensive player. The sparkplug second baseman represented the AL in the 1987 Midsummer Classic, when he joined pitcher Mark Langston to give Seattle two All-Stars for the first time. By the end of the year, he had tied the Big League mark with 12 assists in a game and set the M's single-season record with 60 steals — he now ranks third on the team's career stolen base list with 228, behind Julio Cruz and Ichiro Suzuki. Reynolds, who made the All-Star team again the next year, also won three Gold Glove Awards from 1988–90.

More than stats, though, Reynolds was special to long-suffering Seattle fans because of his boundless enthusiasm for the game. He enjoyed playing and he clearly wanted everyone around him, in the stands and on the field, to join him in that.

As respected as he was as a player, he was no less regarded for his off-field charity work. Recently he has earned the same type of acclaim as a featured analyst on MLB Network.

Seattle's playoff history includes some signature moments. In 1995, the M's were boosted by Jay Buhner's 11th-inning homer in Game 3 of the ALCS (near photo, right), which gave them a 2-games-to-1 lead over the Indians. Earlier, Luis Sojo's bases-clearing double in a one-game playoff against the Angels — which Sojo scored on after an error by pitcher Mark Langston — sealed the AL West crown for Seattle.

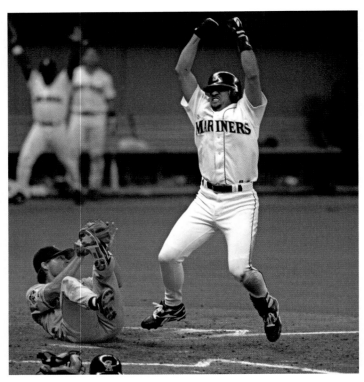

MAKING A RUN

People say they nearly choked away their playoff berth, but perhaps the 1995 Mariners simply preferred the more dramatic route. After the California Angels tied the Mariners atop the AL West on the season's final day, the two teams needed a one-game playoff, which Seattle won easily. Then, in Game 5 of the Division Series against the Yankees, the M's faced a one-run, 11th-inning deficit that stood to end their season. But Edgar Martinez, with a wave of his magic wand, doubled home Joey Cora and Ken Griffey Jr. on a mad dash to send the Mariners to the ALCS. The good karma only lasted as far as the League Championship Series, where the Indians defeated the M's in six games. Seattle got back to the playoffs in 1997 and 2000, losing in the Division Series and ALCS, respectively, but it was in 2001 that the club really made its mark in grand fashion.

After losing three of the greatest players in franchise history over a three-year span, the last thing the team expected was to tie the Big League record for most regular-season wins. But that's just what the 2001 Mariners did, matching the Cubs' 95-year-old mark after losing Randy Johnson in '98, Griffey in 2000 and Alex Rodriguez in '01.

With career years from Bret Boone, Mike Cameron, Aaron Sele and Paul Abbott; solid seasons from stars Edgar Martinez and John Olerud; plus a breakout rookie year from Ichiro Suzuki, Seattle took the AL West, topping Wild Card–winning Oakland by 14 games. The team's defense was key, as the Mariners turned 73 percent of balls put in play into outs, a mark that far and away led the Majors. Pitcher Aaron Sele summed it up when he told the *Los Angeles Times*, "The way our defense is playing, you can be real aggressive with guys and come after them even when you're behind in the count."

Ichiro's impact cannot be understated. In 2001 he hit .350 with 242 base knocks and 56 steals, becoming just the second man to be named MVP and Rookie of the Year in the same season. Over the next decade, he would club at least 200 hits in 10 straight years, claiming the single-season hits record in 2004. "It's spooky, the way Ichiro hits. There's an elegance that cannot be explained," wrote Dave Kindred of the *Sporting News*. "It's as if he's not there. It's just the bat. The bat moves, and he moves with it. With Ichiro, it's so easy it's as if he, like us, is a witness to his wonders."

Ultimately, despite their regular-season success, the 2001 Mariners couldn't get past the defending-champion Yankees in the ALCS, bowing out in five games.

 Seattle's Best

927 **RUNS** scored by the 2001 Mariners, tops in the Major Leagues. The Mariners, who tied a record with 116 wins, had a 3.54 team ERA — also the best in the Bigs.

7 **RUNS** scored by the Mariners on April 8, 1977, to record the team's first-ever win. After being shut out in the first two games, Seattle bounced back with 13 hits.

60 **STOLEN BASES** reached by Harold Reynolds in 1987, a franchise record. The second baseman, who played 10 of his 12 years in Seattle, led the Junior Circuit with 11 triples the next season.

.372 **BATTING AVERAGE** posted by Ichiro Suzuki during his record-setting 2004 season. Ichiro rapped 262 hits to win the batting title and break George Sisler's 84-year-old record of 257 base knocks.

56 **HOME RUNS** hit by perennial All-Star outfielder Ken Griffey Jr. in consecutive seasons (1997 and 1998). "The Kid" took home the AL MVP Award in '97.

8 **STRIKEOUTS** recorded by all-time lefty strikeout king Randy Johnson during his June 2, 1990, no-hitter against Detroit. Five years later, Johnson would win the team's first Cy Young Award.

In 1999, the Mariners finally moved out of the Kingdome, and fans flooded to Safeco Field. The park is famed for some offbeat concessions, including the Ichiroll sushi option.

TAMPA BAY RAYS

LTHOUGH THEY'VE OWNED THE worst overall winning percentage among MLB clubs since putting up a .389 mark in their first season in 1998, the Tampa Bay Rays have made it clear they don't intend to hold that title for long. With three playoff appearances in a four-year span from 2008–11, the Rays are firmly established as perennial contenders in the AL East, baseball's toughest division.

The transformation in St. Petersburg, Fla., began after the 2005 season, when 28-year-old wunderkind Andrew Friedman was promoted to executive vice president of baseball operations — a position from which he would effectively serve as the team's general manager. Frequent losing had resulted in high draft picks, which Friedman used on franchise players Evan Longoria and David Price, among others.

In 2008 the Rays' roster featured no .300 hitters, no 15-game winners and just one batter who topped 85 RBI, yet the club made the World Series on the strength of a vastly improved defense and the sure-handed guidance of cerebral skipper Joe Maddon. They lost to the Phillies in a rain-soaked Fall Classic, but the seeds for success had been sown. In 2010 the Rays won 96 games, second-most in the Majors. The following year was even more incredible. On Sept. 3, 2011, Tampa Bay trailed Boston by nine games in the AL Wild Card race. The Rays closed ground until, on the final day of the season, they came back from a 7-0, eighth-inning deficit against the New York Yankees to clinch a playoff spot. Evan Longoria's 12th-inning walk-off winner was one of the most thrilling home runs in baseball history, and provided the young Rays franchise with another signature moment.

WORST TO FIRST

The Rays gave up a 7-0, seventh-inning lead against Boston in Game 5 of the '08 ALCS and also dropped the next game, but they won Game 7 to oust the Red Sox and earn their first trip to the Fall Classic.

After years of futility, things clicked when GM Andrew Friedman and Manager Joe Maddon took over in 2006. Friedman applied a steady, analytical approach in the front office and Maddon did the same on the field. "He's very calm, quiet and trusting," pitcher James Shields said of Maddon. "Sometimes, you have a manager who yells at you every night, but he doesn't do that. He'll sit you down and talk to you and teach you."

Before getting to that point, though, the Rays reaped the sole perk of finishing in last place: years of high draft picks. And during their first 10 years, the Rays certainly took advantage of that bounty. By the early 2000s, the Rays, it seemed, had become expert talent evaluators. They nabbed Rocco Baldelli in 2000, B.J. Upton in '02 and Delmon Young in '03.

But the two biggest coups came in 2006 and '07, when Tampa Bay drafted Evan Longoria and David Price, respectively. Both played a part in the Rays' success in 2008. In April, after just six Big League games, Longoria signed a long-term, multi-million dollar contract. And the 23-year-old third baseman eased any doubts about

the investment with 27 homers and AL Rookie of the Year honors. The scouting had paid off, and in 2008 the Rays shot all the way from last place to AL champs.

It was in that ALCS that Price caught the nation's eye as well. He had pitched in just five regular-season games, and carried a no-hitter into the fifth inning of his only Big League start. Soon he earned the win in Game 2 of the ALCS with an extra-inning relief stint. In Game 7, Price stepped up as the Rays' closer. He proceeded to strike out three batters — each of whom represented the tying run — holding off Boston to win the pennant.

"Holding off" is an accurate descriptor; the Rays held a 3-games-to-1 series lead in the ALCS, but blew a 7-0, seventh-inning lead in Game 5 to lose, 8-7. Game 6 was tighter, but Boston still prevailed, 4-2, to force a decisive seventh game. A brilliant start by Matt Garza and tight-rope relief work preserved the 3-1 Rays win in the finale, and Tampa Bay punched a ticket to the franchise's first-ever World Series. The result of that Series — a loss to the Phillies in five games — obviously left Rays fans wanting more. And yet, little doubt remained that this worst-to-first journey had been worth every second, and a new era of baseball was dawning in Tampa.

"MADDON WANTS YOU TO FOCUS ON WHAT YOU CAN DO WELL AND TRIES TO PUT YOU IN THOSE POSITIONS TO SUCCEED." —*BEN ZOBRIST*

AGAINST THE GRAIN

Rays skipper Joe Maddon goes against The Book, the unwritten guide to managing a Major League Baseball game. He relishes being a contrarian. Doing things differently than everyone else, he feels, gives him an edge over the competition.

The Rays employ a cadre of skilled analysts, several of whom earned their stripes working for sabermetric think tanks like Baseball Prospectus and The Hardball Times. If anyone has an idea that he thinks can help the team, Maddon welcomes it. If the idea is counter-intuitive or untested, that doesn't bother Maddon — as long as the thinking behind it is sound.

At the heart of the Rays' approach is their embrace of technology. The manager is a big advocate of customized, small-ball pitching machines. If hitters can track a tennis ball going up to 140 mph, Maddon's thinking goes, then they'll have an easier time following a 90-mph fastball thrown to them in a game. Evan Longoria, for

one, has taken to the machines, sharpening his already strong batting eye.

Above all else, Maddon stresses a healthy balance between working hard and having fun. He dreams up casualwear themes that let the players express themselves on road trips. The outfits, meant to be fun, emphasize a little risk-taking and foster team-building.

The best way to make life pleasant for a ballplayer to come to work is to win, and the Rays have done just that since he took over in 2006, with two division crowns and two other contending seasons in his first six years. Maddon believes that if you foster a positive work environment, players will feel better about themselves and their jobs, even when wins are tougher to find.

"He always wants you to focus on what you can do well and tries to put you in those positions to succeed," said Rays second baseman/outfielder Ben Zobrist. "I think you appreciate that as a player, especially in times when you're not playing so well. He's probably the most positive-thinking manager I've ever played for."

Maddon (center) adopted a cerebral approach to the game, going against traditional beliefs if he didn't agree with them. Players such as Longoria have responded.

Fans at Tropicana Field (below) tolerated several seasons of finishing in the American League East basement, but uber-talented players started to come along and, suddenly, the Rays became a perennial contender. Longoria's arrival in the Bigs led to an All-Star selection and Rookie of the Year honors in 2008. On the final day of the 2011 season, he hit a walk-off homer against the Yankees (above) to get the Rays into the playoffs.

THE CORNERSTONE

When he was younger, Evan Longoria would drive down Orange Freeway in Southern California, pass by Angel Stadium of Anaheim and tell himself that someday he would get a chance to play on that field.

"I loved Percy [Troy Percival]," said Longoria. "I loved watching Chuck Finley, Tim Salmon, Garret Anderson and Gary DiSarcina. They had some good teams there when I was growing up."

It seemed like a dream that might never come true. The Downey, Calif., native didn't receive any scholarship offers to play college baseball right out of high school and landed with Rio Hondo Junior College before eventually getting a scholarship to Long Beach State as a sophomore. That's when his career took off.

Three years later, that same once-unheralded player became the top position player taken in the 2006 draft. Tampa Bay executives breathed a huge sigh of relief when they found out at 2 a.m. on the eve of the draft that the infielder would be available with the third pick.

A young player who rose to stardom immediately, Longoria made a huge impact as soon as he came up for the start of the 2008 season. In that campaign, he led his club to its first American League pennant and World

Series appearance, picking up All-Star and Rookie of the Year accolades following the season. In 2009, the former first-round draft pick smashed 33 home runs and 113 RBI, again made the All-Star roster for the Junior Circuit and nabbed both the Gold Glove and Silver Slugger awards for his outstanding defense at third base and his slugging prowess, respectively.

The third baseman has had plenty of memorable experiences in his short career. Take his first All-Star Game, for example; Longoria told locker-mate Manny Ramirez that he was trying to enjoy the experience because he didn't know if he would ever play in another Midsummer Classic. Ramirez's response? "If you think like that, you'll never be back."

Now Longoria is using his Southern California upbringing and attitude to help turn his Major League dream into an All-Star reality.

"It's not enough anymore just to have a winning record," Longoria said during the 2010 season. "We've done some awesome things and we can do more. There are a lot of good things that can come from this team. We have a lot of great young players and that would be my hope — that we can keep those guys around and continue to build.

"We're going to be pretty good for a long time."

TB Rays of Light

31 WINS, the improvement in the Rays' record from 2007 (66-96) to their division-winning 2008 campaign (97-65). Tampa won the AL East by two games over Boston that year.

45,369 FANS turned out for Tampa Bay's first-ever game on March 31, 1998. The Rays' Wilson Alvarez threw the team's first pitch, but the home squad would eventually fall to the Detroit Tigers, 11-6.

239 STRIKEOUTS recorded by 23-year-old Scott Kazmir in 2007, tops in the American League. Kazmir went 13-9 and led the Junior Circuit with 34 starts.

8 RUNS scored by the Rays in the first game of the 2004 season on March 30. In front of 55,000 fans in Tokyo, Japan, Tampa Bay opened the campaign with a win over the Yankees.

46 HOME RUNS belted by first baseman Carlos Pena in 2007, besting the team's single-season club record by 12 longballs. The Rays had acquired Pena as a free agent prior to the season.

27 HOMERS hit by 22-year-old third baseman Evan Longoria in his first 448 Big League at-bats. Longoria won the 2008 AL Rookie of the Year Award for his efforts.

TEXAS RANGERS

ONE OF BASEBALL'S INITIAL TWO expansion teams (along with the Angels), the Washington Senators — not to be confused with the first incarnation that moved to Minnesota and became the Twins — played just 11 years in the nation's capital before moving to Arlington, Texas, and becoming the Rangers in 1972. The Senators never finished better than fourth place in D.C., but gentle giant Frank Howard — who won AL home run titles in 1968 and '70 — remains a beloved figure in Washington even today.

The Rangers' watershed moment was the signing of native Texan Nolan Ryan before the 1989 season. In the 23 years following his signing, the club won at a .506 clip, made five playoff appearances and earned two AL pennants, with the Ryan Express himself serving as team president for the AL crowns. It was Ryan's late-career exploits, though, that made the biggest impression. From the ages of 42–45, Ryan won two strikeout titles, hurled his sixth and seventh no-hitters, recorded his 300th win and 5,000th strikeout, and posted a 3.30 ERA that was 20 percent better than the league average.

Texas's postseason teams of the 1990s featured Gold Glove catcher Ivan Rodriguez as the foundation — and the aging Pudge returned to Texas in 2009 to mentor a young pitching staff on the brink of success. In 2010 and '11 the Rangers won back-to-back AL pennants with a loaded roster that included five-tool outfielder Josh Hamilton — the 2010 AL MVP Award recipient — 30/30 man Ian Kinsler, hard-throwing closer Neftali Feliz and exuberant young shortstop Elvis Andrus. On two excruciating occasions, they came within one strike of winning the 2011 World Series before falling to St. Louis. Still, with skipper Ron Washington keeping the clubhouse loose, Texas has become a perennial contender.

KINGS OF THE AMERICAN LEAGUE

In the days leading up to the 2010 Fall Classic, it was hard not to feel excited for two fan bases chasing something they had never before held. The faithful in San Francisco and Texas both entered the World Series without their teams ever having won a championship, and their excitement was obvious. The experience — if not the conclusion — was especially sweet for the Rangers' new ownership group, headed by Hall of Fame pitcher Nolan Ryan. And while the road to the World Series is a long one, the front office has inspired confidence in the team's fan base for long-term success.

The Rangers' 2010 playoff run included a five-game Division Series win over the Rays, spearheaded by Cliff Lee, and a six-game ALCS triumph over the defending champion Yankees. Their fortune ran out there, as ultimately the Giants' pitching held the Rangers in check over the course of five games. It didn't help that the once-indefatigable Lee suddenly turned into a pumpkin, but the big picture was that a 2010 championship was simply not meant to be. Coming so far only to fall short left a bitter taste in the mouths of Rangers players, and those who would return to the club the following year had just one thing on their minds.

And so the Rangers came back with a vengeance in 2011. Steamrolling to 96 regular season wins with new third baseman Adrian Beltre but without Lee, the Rangers comfortably won the AL West and set their sights on rectifying their unfinished business. A rematch with the Rays in the ALDS proved to be something akin to deja vu, as Texas advanced in four games. Then came a matchup with the dangerous Detroit Tigers, led by the soon-to-be Cy Young– and MVP Award–winner Justin Verlander. Rain wreaked havoc on pitching matchups,

but the power bat of Nelson Cruz could not be dampened. The right fielder hit an LCS-record six homers — including a walk-off grand slam in Game 2 — en route to claiming ALCS MVP Award honors.

Unfortunately, the outcome of the 2011 World Series was no different than it had been in '10 for Texas. To be sure, the Rangers came much closer to actually claiming the title than they did in 2010 — within one strike on two separate occasions — but an unforgettable Game 6 turned the tide of the Series in favor of the St. Louis Cardinals, who would eventually claim the seventh game, as well.

ALL ABOARD THE RYAN EXPRESS

Nolan Ryan was frightening to face during his high school days in east Texas. Armed with an incredible heater — and seemingly no idea of where it was going — he was said to have broken one opponent's arm and another's helmet on consecutive pitches. The New York Mets took a chance that he could harness his power, though, and selected him in the 12th round of the amateur draft in 1965.

As a Minor Leaguer, Ryan remained the prototypical gunslinger. "A guy either had the skill and timing to hit the heater or he struck out," Ryan would later say of the challenge he presented to batters. Few could hit it, and by 1968, Ryan was in the Big Leagues to kick off his long and historic career. Like numerous hard throwers before him, he developed breaking pitches and became much better at locating his offerings to morph into a more complete pitcher. Of course, it wasn't always perfect. Power pitchers like Ryan — although, really, there's only one Nolan Ryan — often feature high walk totals along with their K's. In fact, Ryan is one of just two pitchers in history to walk 200 batters in a season, Bob Feller being the other. And Ryan is the only one to top the 200–free pass mark twice.

Even with that streak of wildness, Ryan dealt for 27 seasons, becoming the game's all-time strikeout leader by a wide margin — and the first to cross 5,000 K's, which he did as a member of the Rangers in 1989. He was a key contributor for the world champion Miracle Mets in 1969, when he pitched 9.1 innings of World Series relief with 10 strikeouts. Four years later, this time with the California Angels, he threw his first of a Major League–record seven no-hitters on May 15 in Kansas City. In two hours and 20 minutes, he issued just three walks and struck out 12.

Despite all his years in cosmopolitan locales like New York and California, his fans always saw him as a throwback — a hard-charging but soft-spoken country boy unafraid of confrontation. It didn't hurt that Ryan could still light up the radar gun late in his playing days, thriving into his mid-40s while pitching for the Astros and Rangers in his native Lone Star State.

Mike Napoli (center) hit a three-run shot to propel Texas to a Game 4 win in the 2011 World Series. A strike away from victory in Game 6, Texas would end up falling short against St. Louis in a seven-game Fall Classic.

"A GUY EITHER HAD THE SKILL AND TIMING TO HIT THE HEATER OR HE STRUCK OUT."
—NOLAN RYAN

Rodriguez established himself as the best fielding catcher ever during his Rangers tenure. Over the course of his career, Pudge won 13 Gold Gloves, the most for a backstop in history. That total included a stretch of 10 straight from 1992–2001.

PUDGE

"It's the best season I've seen, all around, by a catcher," All-Star backstop Sandy Alomar said of Ivan Rodriguez's 1999 MVP campaign. It was "all around" great because, in addition to his prowess at the plate, Rodriguez played superb defense behind it.

The anchor of the first-place Texas Rangers that year, "Pudge" caught 141 games, striking fear in opposing base runners with his lethal throwing arm.

That one season was no outlier, either. In his storied career, which spanned more than two decades, Rodriguez collected, 13 Gold Glove Awards, seven Silver Slugger Awards and 14 All-Star Game nods in addition to that 1999 MVP Award. Although not quite Johnny Bench with the bat, Rodriguez's offensive prowess was impressive nonetheless, especially at a position that isn't often rife with premium talent with the stick.

Pudge spent the first 12 seasons of his career in Texas, where he won the majority of his accolades. What he never did collect, however, was a World Series trophy. In those years, the Rangers made the postseason three times, losing in the Division Series in each instance. A deep playoff run was a foreign concept to Rodriguez, until the 2003 season. Leaving the only Big League home he had ever known to sign a one-year deal with the Florida Marlins, Rodriguez played a major part in the Marlins' improbable run to a World Series championship, including making a play at the plate to secure a Division Series win for the Fish.

T Lone Stars

44 HOMERS hit by Washington Senators slugger Frank Howard in both 1968 and 1970. Howard posted 40-plus homers and 100-plus RBI in all three seasons from 1968–70.

96 WINS posted by the 2011 Rangers, a franchise record. The team would go on to win the AL pennant only to lose in seven games in the World Series to the Cardinals.

3 GRAND SLAMS crushed by Larry Parrish from July 4–10, 1982, setting a Major League record for a calendar week. Over that time, he hit .290 with four home runs and 17 RBI.

27 CONSECUTIVE BATTERS retired by Kenny Rogers on July 28, 1994, in the first perfect game ever thrown by a Rangers pitcher. Rogers did it in a 4-0 win over the Angels.

30 RUNS scored by the Rangers on Aug. 22, 2007, in a record-breaking 30-3 win over the Baltimore Orioles. To get there, Texas compiled 29 hits, including six home runs.

10 GOLD GLOVES won by Ivan Rodriguez as the Rangers' star backstop. "Pudge" also won an MVP Award in 1999 for Texas, the year he hit .332 with 35 homers and 113 RBI.

TORONTO BLUE JAYS

W HEN THE EXPANSION Toronto Blue Jays debuted in 1977, they showed the baseball world something it had literally never seen before. The first game in franchise history, held in a modified football stadium, was delayed by a blizzard blowing gusts of snow from Lake Ontario a block away. After a Zamboni was used to clear the infield, the Jays defeated the White Sox, 9-5.

Fans loved their baseball in the frozen North, though, and Toronto became a model for how to build an expansion franchise into a perennial contender. Boasting what was considered the best outfield of the era — Jesse Barfield, George Bell and Lloyd Moseby — the Jays won 99 games and the AL East title in 1985, just their ninth season. Toronto finished at least 10 games over .500 every year from 1983–93. Fans loved the exciting style of Tony Fernandez, who in 1986 stole 25 bases, won a Gold Glove and broke MLB's single-season record for hits by a shortstop with 212 — a mark that has since been broken.

Toronto captured back-to-back World Series titles — its first two ever — in 1992 and '93 while setting attendance records in the futuristic SkyDome. GM Pat Gillick constructed a lineup that was hailed as one of the greatest in baseball history. Of the nine regulars in 1993, three of them — Roberto Alomar, Paul Molitor and Rickey Henderson — were Hall of Famers in their prime, while five of the other six earned at least one All-Star nod during their careers. The lineup was so stacked that Manager Cito Gaston was forced to bench AL batting champ John Olerud for one of the games they played at the Philadelphia Phillies' home ballpark during the '93 World Series, but the Jays nonetheless captured the championship on Joe Carter's unforgettable walk-off winner in Game 6.

BACK TO BACK

The Blue Jays' 1992 world title (left) was one of the great moments in Canadian sports history, but it couldn't touch the scene that fans saw the next year, when Carter's World Series–clinching homer off Williams set off a celebration around the bases for the ages.

When the first World Series took place in 1903, the handful of Big League teams that spread across the Northeast and the Midwest of the United States hardly justified its ambitious moniker. The Fall Classic, though, became a truly international event when it moved outside the United States for the first time in 1992, thanks to the Toronto Blue Jays.

The Jays topped the Oakland Athletics in the ALCS that year to earn their first World Series berth, and when Toronto hosted the Atlanta Braves on Oct. 20 for Game 3, SkyDome became the site of the first World Series contest played outside the United States. It was a dramatic Series debut, ending in the bottom of the ninth when Toronto's Candy Maldonado snapped a 2-2 tie with an RBI single, giving the Jays a 3-2 walk-off win. Toronto won the next night, too, but was unable to put the Braves away in Game 5, falling, 7-2.

The Jays battled through a roller-coaster Game 6 in Atlanta. Toronto coughed up a lead in the bottom of the ninth, as the Braves rallied to tie. In the top of the 11th, the Blue Jays scored twice, but it wasn't until Mike Timlin fielded an Otis Nixon bunt and threw him out with one run having already scored, a runner at third and two outs that Toronto could celebrate. The 4-3 win

brought the Commissioner's Trophy out of the United States for the first time.

The following year was a fitting encore. The Jays were back to defend their title against an unlikely opponent. After finishing last in the NL East in 1992, the Phillies held off the Expos to win the division in 1993 and then stunned the Braves in six games in the National League Championship Series. Toronto defeated the White Sox in the ALCS, then took a 3-games-to-1 lead in the World Series before Curt Schilling renewed the Phillies' faith with a five-hit, 2-0 shutout in Game 5.

Actually, the Phils had every reason to believe they were headed for a seventh game, having scored five runs in the seventh inning of Game 6 to take a 6-5 lead. As the game entered the final inning, the burden of extending the Series fell to Philly reliever Mitch Williams, who sandwiched a walk and single around a fly out to start the ninth. But as Williams delivered a 2-2 pitch to Joe Carter, a down-and-in slider that did little except invite devastation, the weight was about to become too much.

Carter didn't just connect with it — he crushed it. And he didn't just hit a ninth-inning home run; he ended the '93 World Series with his walk-off, three-run blast in Game 6. Carter propelled the Blue Jays to a memorable 8-6 victory over the Phillies and gave Toronto its second straight world championship.

NORTH OF THE BORDER

When the Toronto Blue Jays set out to design a new ball-park, they desired the best of both worlds. The franchise wanted the option to play outdoors in the fresh air, but also wanted the playing field to be protected in the case of inclement weather. The Blue Jays achieved both goals, revolutionizing stadium construction with a retractable-roof dome. SkyDome (now called Rogers Centre), which opened its doors on June 5, 1989, was a state-of-the-art facility. It put to shame the franchise's previous home, Exhibition Stadium, which was a football venue that had been retrofitted for baseball when the Blue Jays joined the American League 12 years earlier.

The 22-million-pound roof at Rogers Centre — which takes 20 minutes to open or close — features three sliding and rotating panels that are stacked up with a fourth when the roof is open. The club's investment, $600 million (Canadian), was worth every loonie; the Blue Jays set Big League attendance records as a result, drawing more than 4 million fans each year from 1991–93.

When the roof is open, the seats along the third-base line at Rogers Centre (nee SkyDome) offer a picture-perfect view of a famous Toronto landmark, the CN Tower. When closed — a process that takes about 20 minutes — the roof keeps the fans protected from Toronto's sometimes frigid temperatures.

BELL DID HIS SHARE TO KEEP THE '87 JAYS IN THE HUNT, HITTING 47 HOME RUNS, INCLUDING NINE IN AUGUST. HE ALSO PILED UP 16 GAME-WINNING RBI.

Although his team was knocked from contention in the final weekend of '87, MVP voters still recognized that had it not been for Bell's excellence throughout the year, Toronto's final series would have been meaningless.

Bell was a precursor to several fantastic Blue Jays sluggers, including Joe Carter and Shawn Green. But the granddaddy of them all was Puerto Rican masher Carlos Delgado, who played for the Jays from 1994–2004.

Starting his career as a catcher, Delgado moved to first base and became the Blue Jays' all-time leader in home runs, RBI, OPS and numerous other categories. He drove in 100 runs nine times, culminating in a Major League–leading figure of 145 in 2003. He hit 30 homers each of his last eight years with the club, and in 2003 he slugged a record-tying four in one game.

And, of course, he accomplished all of this with an exuberant smile on his face. "One of baseball's most admired gentlemen — friendly, mature," *The Washington Post*'s Thomas Boswell wrote. "Such players exist, with Delgado as a prime example." In 2006 he was named the recipient of the Roberto Clemente Award, which honors an athlete's commitment to excellence on the field as well as community service. The slugger was one of the game's most eloquent and personable stars, and wasn't afraid to stand up — or sit down — for what he believed in, such as when he protested the Iraq war in 2004 by heading into the clubhouse during renditions of "God Bless America."

HEAVYWEIGHTS

Bell made two All-Star teams and won an MVP Award during his nine seasons with the Blue Jays.

A powerful outfielder in the Junior Circuit, George Bell, the first Dominican-born player to win the MVP Award, did it all for the Toronto Blue Jays in 1987. "He's got a bad shoulder from carrying the rest of the ballclub all summer," quipped Detroit Manager Sparky Anderson.

Although the Jays eventually fell short of the post-season — to Anderson's Tigers — the left fielder had done his share to keep them in the hunt. Bell hit a club record 47 home runs — including nine in August — batted .308 and topped the AL with 134 RBI. He also piled up 16 game-winning RBI and 15 assists in the field.

Such production might have been impossible when Bell first signed in 1974 since he weighed in at just 154 pounds. But after years of hard work he came into the '87 season 40 pounds heavier. And pitchers paid the price.

 Canadian Currency

213 **HITS** clubbed by Tony Fernandez in 1986. In the process, Fernandez became the first Blue Jay with 200-plus hits in a season. Club veteran Vernon Wells later topped him in 2003 with 215 on the year.

9 **RUNS** scored by the Blue Jays in their first game. On April 7, 1977, Toronto topped the Chicago White Sox, 9-5, in front of 44,649 in freezing temperatures at home.

35 **STEALS** recorded by Shawn Green in 1998. He also slugged 35 home runs to join the 30/30 club. The following season, Green belted 42 homers.

99 **WINS** posted by Toronto in 1985 under skipper Bobby Cox. The total remains a club record, ahead of the team's two World Series seasons (1992 and 1993).

.363 **BATTING AVERAGE** recorded by John Olerud to win the 1993 batting title. Teammates Paul Molitor (.332) and Roberto Alomar (.326) finished second and third, respectively, that year.

5 **GOLD GLOVE AWARDS** won by perennial All-Star second baseman Roberto Alomar in five consecutive seasons from 1991–95. He would finish his career with 10 Gold Gloves.

Delgado wielded a fearsome bat from the left side, which allowed him to dominate AL pitchers for years. Yet his lasting reputation is as much a result of his work in the community as for his offensive stroke.

WASHINGTON NATIONALS

ALTHOUGH BASEBALL IN MONTREAL is likely remembered for its ignominious end more than anything else, *Les Expos* were a thriving and successful franchise for most of their existence in Quebec, finishing .500 or better 14 times from 1979–96. Playing their early seasons on a diamond nestled inside a city park with a swimming pool behind the right-field fence, fans fell in love with redheaded outfielder Rusty Staub, who they dubbed *Le Grand Orange*.

The loaded Expos of the 1980s featured two Hall of Famers — Gary Carter and Andre Dawson — plus Tim Raines, who at his astonishing peak was better than either of them. Raines was arguably the greatest baserunner of all time, swiping 808 bases at an 85 percent success rate (even all-time stolen base king Rickey Henderson succeeded at just an 81 percent rate). He also won the 1986 batting title while topping a .400 on-base percentage three years in a row. The Raines-led Expos made their lone playoff appearance in 1981 but lost to the Dodgers in the NLCS on a heartbreaking Rick Monday homer.

The 1990s saw Montreal stock its roster with some of the best young talent in the game, including pitcher Pedro Martinez and sluggers Larry Walker and Moises Alou, but a strike ended the 1994 season in August, just as the Expos were boasting MLB's best record. Despite the emergence of five-tool outfielder Vladimir Guerrero, the team and its fan base never really recovered, and the club moved to Washington in 2005. The early years in the nation's capital were tough ones — the Nats finished last in five of their first six seasons — but fan interest was high thanks to the opening of the gorgeous Nationals Park and the arrival of heralded draft pick Stephen Strasburg.

A heralded prospect and the 2009 No. 1 draft pick, Strasburg quickly became the face of the franchise.

A Hall of Famer, Dawson followed in Willie Mays' footsteps to become just the second player ever to join the 400/300 club, finishing with 438 home runs and 314 steals.

THE HAWK

Despite the fact that the Nationals franchise left Montreal in 2004, a second Expo made the Hall of Fame in 2010. Andre Dawson, the Rookie of the Year in 1977, played with the club through 1986, winning six Gold Glove Awards and three Silver Slugger Awards in Montreal.

Dawson did some incredible things on the baseball field with the Expos, Cubs, Red Sox and Marlins. His portfolio included eight All-Star appearances, 438 home runs and 314 stolen bases. That power-speed combination allowed him to join the exclusive 400/300 club, a small fraternity currently comprised of just Dawson, Willie Mays, Barry Bonds and Alex Rodriguez.

But when Dawson's former teammates reflect on his career and the character traits that stood out most, they routinely focus on his pregame routine, when he would spend two hours on an exercise machine getting his knees

in condition to play, and the post-game, when he needed almost as long to recover from the damage caused to them by Montreal's rock-hard artificial playing surface.

Dawson suffered his first knee injury as a high school football player in Florida, and the discomfort eventually became so acute that he required pain medication to play and even contemplated retirement at age 25. By the time he entered the Hall of Fame in 2010, Dawson had reportedly undergone 12 operations, developed arthritis in both knees and required two knee replacement surgeries on the left one.

"He inspired me," said Tim Raines, Dawson's teammate in Montreal from 1979–86. "You'd see him in a game and think there was nothing wrong with him, and then after games the guy couldn't even walk. He went through more ice than anybody ever went through in their entire lives. I'm surprised there's still ice around, as much as this guy put on his body."

STARTING OFF WITH A BANG

During its formative years, the new iteration of the Washington Nationals played its home games in the cavernous RFK Stadium, which previously housed the NFL's Washington Redskins. The inaugural Nationals club gave its fans an immediate contender, as the Nats stayed in the thick of things for most of the year. Through August, they had a 69-65 record, although they would ultimately finish with an 81-81 mark, nine games behind the first-place Atlanta Braves. But the ensuing years saw the Nationals repeatedly post sub-.500 records.

To be fair, that belies the progress the club has made since bottoming out with consecutive 59-win seasons in 2008 and '09. Helped along by the top draft picks that came with those poor records, the Nationals drafted phenoms Stephen Strasburg and Bryce Harper in consecutive years, adding name recognition, potential star power and, most importantly, optimism for the future.

On June 8, 2010, Strasburg stormed onto the scene, arriving in the Majors to a hype so deafening, the rookie sensation couldn't possibly live up to it. Or so some thought. Instead, he exceeded it, fanning 14 Pirates in seven innings of work. Before undergoing season-ending Tommy John surgery, the young flamethrower posted a 2.91 ERA and 92 strikeouts in 12 starts, demonstrating that, when healthy, his arm is golden. Indeed, Strasburg confirmed that when he returned at the end of 2011, posting a 1.50 ERA and striking out 24 while walking just two in five starts.

Strasburg is merely following in the footsteps of the new Nationals' first truly homegrown star, Ryan Zimmerman. Zimmerman christened Nationals Park — and Opening Day on America's shores — with a walk-off home run against the Braves on March 30, 2008. Zimmerman, the fourth overall pick of the 2005 draft and Rookie of the Year runner-up in 2006, made a winner out of Jon Rauch, who had surrendered the game-tying run in the top of the ninth after Paul Lo Duca's passed ball. The homer was the first of 20 for Zimmerman in 2008.

Another Zimmermann — this one named Jordan and with an extra "N" at the end — made his Big League debut with the Nationals in 2009. The second round pick made his first Major League start at Nationals Park, earning the win with a 3-2 victory, also over the Braves. Like Strasburg, Zimmermann underwent Tommy John surgery — in August 2009 — but came back looking better than ever, and gave Nats fans the hope of a dominant one-two punch in the rotation.

The one who may end up making the biggest splash of all Nationals, though, is Bryce Harper, a catcher-turned-outfielder who was drafted as a 17-year-old phenom and who made his pro debut in 2011. Moving from Class-A to Double-A ball as an 18-year-old, Harper slugged .501 and mashed 17 home runs in 109 games across both levels.

With a view of the Capitol Building in the background, Zimmerman made some noise at the opening of Nationals Park on March 30, 2008. The club's home-grown star hit a walk-off home run to push the team past Atlanta.

 Capital Gains

 With the Nationals taking on the defending NL champion and intra-division rival Philadelphia Phillies on Opening Day 2010, U.S. President Barack Obama threw out the first pitch in his backyard, Nationals Park.

42 HOME RUNS hit by outfielder Vladimir Guerrero in 1999 to become the first player in club history to hit 40-plus longballs in a season. He bested that mark with 44 the next year.

46 LONGBALLS crushed by Alfonso Soriano in 2006, setting a new club record. Soriano had been acquired via trade from Texas prior to the season.

41 STOLEN BASES reached by Soriano in 2006, to go along with his home run and steals totals. He also piled up a whopping 41 doubles to become the inaugural member of baseball's extremely elite 40/40/40 club.

47 SAVES recorded by Nationals closer Chad Cordero in 2005, tops in the Major Leagues. The former Cal State Fullerton standout also posted a 1.82 ERA that year.

19 COMPLETE GAMES logged by lefty Ross Grimsley in 1978. That season, the first-year Montreal Expo became the first in franchise history to win 20 games (20-11).

2 RUNS scored for Dennis Martinez on July 28, 1991, the day the Expos' hurler tossed a perfect game against the Dodgers. Martinez whiffed five L.A. batters in the process.

"IT DOESN'T MATTER IF THE BALL IS A FOOT OUTSIDE OR HIGH OR IN THE DIRT. IT SEEMS LIKE HIS BAT FINDS A WAY TO GET TO THE BALL."
— *TERRY MULHOLLAND*

VLAD THE IMPALER

Although a language barrier and an overpowering shyness rendered Vladimir Guerrero one of the quietest superstars in modern baseball, there was nothing silent about his talent, his heart or his bat when he played in Montreal. "Vladi is a player you dream of," ex-teammate Pedro Martinez once said. "He's in a class with A-Rod and Manny and any great hitter you can name."

Growing up part of a poor family in the Dominican Republic, Guerrero was so thin at the age of 16 that the Los Angeles Dodgers, who had signed his older brother Wilton, passed on Vladimir because they doubted that he would develop. Montreal scooped him up instead, and his swing-at-everything approach — which worked for him despite convention because he could still crush balls thrown off the plate — made him the franchise's all-time leader in batting average, homers and OPS. In just over seven years with the club, he hit .323 with a .390 OBP, 234 homers, 226 doubles and 123 stolen bases. "It doesn't matter if the ball is a foot outside or a foot high or down in the dirt," opponent Terry Mulholland marveled. "It seems like his bat finds a way to get to the ball."

After several years as the game's best-kept secret in Montreal — where he also made four All-Star teams and won three Silver Slugger Awards — Guerrero signed with the Angels as a free agent in 2004. He was voted the league MVP after his first year in Anaheim and led the Angels to five AL West titles in his six seasons there. He virtually made a career out of terrorizing the Texas Rangers while with the Angels, batting .396 with a 1.127 OPS in 102 career games against the division rival. In 2010, the Rangers did the only thing they could to stop Guerrero: They signed him. At age 35, he hit .300 and drove in 115 runs to help the club reach the World Series for the first time in franchise history.

Guerrero's plate approach may have been unorthodox, but his swing-away style helped earn him plenty of batting accolades.

BIBLIOGRAPHY

BOOKS AND MAGAZINES

Official MLB All-Star Game Program: 1998, 2000, 2001, 2002, 2003, 2004, 2005, 2006, 2007, 2009, 2010, 2011

Mets Magazine: September 2008

Official MLB League Championship Series Program: 2001, 2002, 2005, 2009, 2011

Official MLB World Series Program: 2000, 2001, 2002, 2003, 2004, 2005, 2006, 2007, 2008, 2009, 2010, 2011

Official MLB Yearbook: 2001, 2004, 2005

Fenway Park: 100 Years

Major League Baseball Opus

WEBSITES

www.baseball-almanac.com

www.baseball-reference.com

www.mlb.com

PHOTO CREDITS

JORDAN MEGENHARDT/ARIZONA DIAMONDBACKS/MLB PHOTOS: Cover (Diamondbacks); 8-9

CINDY LOO/BOSTON RED SOX/MLB PHOTOS: Cover (Fenway Park); 32-33; 36-37

OTTO GREULE JR./GETTY IMAGES: Cover (Henderson); 55; 92 (Scott); 126; 156-157; 159 (Stewart); 163; 208; 209

MICHAEL HEIMAN/GETTY IMAGES: Cover (Jeter); 149 (Jeter 2)

JIM McISAAC/GETTY IMAGES: Cover (Lidge/Ruiz); 168-169

ROB CARR/GETTY IMAGES: Cover (Freese); 185

DILIP VISHWANAT/GETTY IMAGES: 2-3; 186-187

MICHAEL ZAGARIS/MLB PHOTOS: 6; 121 (Renteria)

RICH PILLING/MLB PHOTOS: 10 (Arizona's first game); 10 (2001 WS); 52-53; 57 (Jenks); 93 (Bagwell); 94 (Minute Maid Park); 106 (Salmon); 127; 132 (Target Field 3); 134-135; 142-143; 154; 173; 178-179; 222 (Rodriguez); 222 (Mascot); 229; 230-231; 233 (Nation's Capitol); 234; 235

JONATHAN WILLEY/ARIZONA DIAMONDBACKS/MLB PHOTOS: 12; 13

STEPHEN DUNN/GETTY IMAGES: 14-15; 20; 195

NATIONAL BASEBALL HALL OF FAME LIBRARY/MLB PHOTOS: Cover (Tigers); 16 (Smoltz); 17; 22 (Aaron); 23 (Murphy); 24-25 (Sisler); 29 (Ripken); 45 (Caray); 47; 48-49; 54; 56 (Minoso); 64-65; 68-69; 70; 74; 75; 84 (Cobb); 89; 98; 136; 152 (Mantle kneeling); 153 (DiMaggio); 158 (Mack); 180 (Wagner); 228 (Bell)

BRIAN BAHR/GETTY IMAGES: 18-19; 94 (Gipson); 94 (05 NLCS); 95 (Celebration)

STREETER LECKA/GETTY IMAGES: 21

PHOTO FILE/MLB PHOTOS: 26-27 (Camden Yards); 31 (F. Robinson); 31 (B. Robinson); 117 (Snider)

MARK CUNNINGHAM/DETROIT TIGERS/MLB PHOTOS: 28 (Hat); 86-87

MITCHELL LAYTON/WASHINGTON NATIONALS/MLB PHOTOS: 28 (Mascot)

DOUG PENSINGER/GETTY IMAGES: 29; 80 (Fireworks); 122 (Fan); 122 (Ramirez); 201

LOUIS REQEUNA/MLB PHOTOS: 30 (Palmer); 30 (Dobson); 67; 88 (McLain); 107; 128; 141 (Seaver); 144 (Agee); 144 (Celebration); 146-147; 150-151; 152 (Mantle); 176; 180 (Parker); 184

BOSTON RED SOX/MLB PHOTOS: 34 (Williams); 38 (Fenway Park); 39 (Green Monster)

JULIE CORDEIRO/BOSTON RED SOX/MLB PHOTOS: 35; 40 (Green Monster)

BRIAN BABINEAU/BOSTON RED SOX/MLB PHOTOS: 39 (Fenway Park)

MICHAEL IVINS/BOSTON RED SOX/MLB PHOTOS: 40 (Fans)

AP PHOTO: 41; 71; 190 (Dizzy and Daffy); 200; 204

STEPHEN GREEN/CHICAGO CUBS/MLB PHOTOS: 42-43 (Wrigley Field)

LIBRARY OF CONGRESS: 43 (Tinker, Evers and Chance)

RON VESELY/MLB PHOTOS: 44 (Wrigley Field); 58-59; 182-183; 220

JONATHAN DANIEL/GETTY IMAGES: 46, 51 (Fans); 51 (Wrigley Field); 224-225

MATTHEW STOCKMAN/GETTY IMAGES: 50

BRAD MANGIN/MLB PHOTOS: 52-53; 123; 160-161; 218-219; 223

JOHN GRIESHOP/MLB PHOTOS: 57 (Celebration); 66; 73 (Helmet); 73 (Fan); 93 (Biggio)

MLB PHOTOS: 60-61; 88 (Parrish); 92 (Ryan); 96-97; 102; 130-131; 133;

137 (Puckett); 148; 158 (Fox); 159 (Celebration); 166; 171; 174-175; 177; 180 (Stargell); 180 (Kiner); 189; 190 (Cardinals); 191; 196; 226 (Celebration); 226 (Carter)

FOCUS ON SPORT/GETTY IMAGES: 62; 92 (Richard); 113

CINCINNATI REDS/MLB PHOTOS: 63 (Rijo)

JARED WICKERHAM/GETTY IMAGES: 72-73 (Progressive Field)

HARRY HOW/GETTY IMAGES: 76-77; 121 (Counsell)

JAMIE SCHWABEROW/RICH CLARKSON AND ASSOCIATES: 78; 79

RICH CLARKSON AND ASSOCIATES/MLB PHOTOS: 79 (Walker); 80 (Coors Field)

STEPHEN NOWLAND/RICH CLARKSON AND ASSOCIATES: 81 (Coors Field)

CHRISTIAN PETERSEN/GETTY IMAGES: 81 (07 NLCS); 203; 205

LEON HALIP/GETTY IMAGES: 85

DOUG BENC/GETTY IMAGES: 90-91

JAMIE SQUIRE/GETTY IMAGES: 98

KANSAS CITY ROYALS/MLB PHOTOS: 100-101 (Kauffman Stadium); 103 (85 WS)

RONALD MODRA/SPORTS ILLUSTRATED/GETTY IMAGES: 103 (Orta)

AL BELLO/GETTY IMAGES: 104-105; 145

LOS ANGELES ANGELS/MLB PHOTOS: 106 (Celebration); 108 (Scioscia)

JOHN WILLIAMSON/MLB PHOTOS: 109 (Salmon)

DEBORA ROBINSON/MLB PHOTOS: 109 (Rodriguez)

CURT GUNTHER/KEYSTONE/GETTY IMAGES: 110-111

LA DODGERS/MLB PHOTOS: 112 (Valenzuela 2); 116 (Gibson)

JEFF GROSS/GETTY IMAGES: 114-115

MIAMI MARLINS/MLB PHOTOS: 118-119 (Marlins); 120 (New Stadium)

MIKE EHRMANN/GETTY IMAGES: 120 (Mascot); 141 (Mascot)

DENIS BANCROFT/MIAMI MARLINS/MLB PHOTOS: 122 (Celebration)

SCOTT BOEHM/GETTY IMAGES: 124-125; 129 (Gallardo); 129 (Miller Park)

RICK STEWART/GETTY IMAGES: 137 (Morris); 232

T.G. HIGGINS/GETTY IMAGES: 138-139; 140 (Dykstra); 140 (Celebration)

ROB TRINGALI/MLB PHOTOS: 155

JED JACOBSOHN/GETTY IMAGES: 162; 167 (Jenkins); 167 (Utley); 202 (AT&T Park); 210 (Buhner)

CHRIS TROTMAN/GETTY IMAGES: 164-165; 170

PHILADELPHIA PHILLIES/MLB PHOTOS: 172 (Alexander)

ELSA/GETTY IMAGES: 188; 214 (Trophy)

DONALD MIRALLE/GETTY IMAGES: 192-193

CRAIG JONES/GETTY IMAGES: 194

EZRA SHAW/GETTY IMAGES: 198-199

TRAVIS LINDQUIST/GETTY IMAGES: 202-203

JEFF GROSS/GETTY IMAGES: 206-207

BEN VANHOUTEN/MLB PHOTOS: 210 (Sojo); 211

SKIP MILOS/TAMPA BAY RAYS/MLB PHOTOS: 212-213; 215; 216 (Tropicana Field)

STEVEN KOVICH: 214 (Celebration)

J. MERIC/GETTY IMAGES: 216 (Longoria)

CHARLES SONNENBLICK/GETTY IMAGES: 217

JOHN CORDES/LOS ANGELES ANGELS/MLB PHOTOS: 221

BRAD WHITE/GETTY IMAGES: 227 (Rogers Center)

DAVE SANDFORD/GETTY IMAGES: 227 (Rogers Center)

DREW HALLOWELL/GETTY IMAGES: 233 (Zimmerman)

INDEX